Frontier

Published by Barrelhouse Books
Baltimore, MD

www.barrelhousemag.com

Published in the United States of America

ISBN 13: 979-8-9850089-3-7

First Edition

Cover design: Shanna Compton
Page design: Adam Robinson

Frontier

A Memoir and a Ghost Story

Erica Stern

For Jonah, Isaac, and Nathan

"you breathe differently down here."

—Adrienne Rich, "Diving Into the Wreck"

Chicago

Don't worry, I'm not in labor, **I reassure the driver. We make** quick eye contact in the rearview mirror. I want to spare him the image of water breaking, gushing onto his clean upholstery. *Just a routine visit,* I say.

The story I think I'll tell about this day: how I stood in the shower, put a hand to my back where a tightness stretched across, and thought, *nah, that's not it.* Got out and dressed. Sent Jed off to work before climbing in this car.

How silly! I'll think, as I tell the story, inserting a laugh at just the right moment. Shaking my head in disbelief at my naivete. *Little did I know*, I'll say, before moving on to the moment when I realize I'm already in labor.

This is how women learn to narrate their lives.

In the prenatal yoga studio days before, the instructor said, *send your breath energy and your love energy to your baby.* There were four of us cycling through sun salutations. Over the past few weeks, due dates had come and gone. First the woman expecting twins, then the one with back pains requiring specialized adjustments for each pose. Now I was left with the largest baby. The instructor flicked on the lights. I felt the other women's eyes follow me as I rose from my mat, rolled it up, walked it to the shelf across the room; I was royalty, albeit of temporary status. They were taking me in before I disappeared into the glowing abyss that waited for us all.

I'd watched the others in this position before me with jealousy and trepidation, relief that it wasn't me and longing for it to be. I gathered clues where I could find them; I scrounged for hints of what might lie in wait. The conversation around birth, in spite of the bare-it-all approach of social media and the "radical honesty" of therapy-speak, remained strangely shrouded. People spoke of their experiences in generalities and cliches, fitting the plot points into a preexisting narrative. They gave details, even gory and personal ones, and still, it felt like they were omitting something crucial. I wanted to know what it felt like to undergo a metamorphosis.

After the driver drops me in front of the hospital's outpatient pavilion, I ride the elevator up to Hematology to have my blood drawn and platelets counted. For weeks now I've been visiting this doctor, the appointments swarming my calendar in black alongside increasingly frequent OB visits. My platelets had begun to plummet as I neared term, a phenomenon, like much of pregnancy, documented but not well-understood. The hematologist prescribed what she called steroid pulses, and said the pills would make me hungry and restless and on edge. But what woman in her eighth month of pregnancy isn't already those things? The timing of the doses was pure guessing game, working backward from my due date to optimize the power of the drugs so my levels might peak when my body decided it was time.

You could still safely have brain surgery with these labs, she reassured on one of my visits to her clinic. She pulled her long black hair back from her face and recounted the successful c-section of another patient whose platelet levels were much lower than mine. I was supposed to be comforted by this story—healthy mom, healthy baby. But the patient had needed to go under general anesthesia and so this planted a fear: that I might be asleep for delivery. I thought it was critical that I remember the moment I transitioned from one kind of person into another. How could I trust that the baby was mine and not an imposter if it was simply deposited in my arms when the meds wore off and I woke, groggy and in pain and with an empty space in my womb but no story of how the thing inside was removed?

I felt that in signing up for pregnancy and parenthood I'd been promised a diaper-commercial birth in which I'd hear a red-faced baby cry, then hold it to my chest to facilitate an endorphin release like a geyser. I saw the Trevi Fountain in my mind's eye, though I only knew it from photographs. Opulent to the point of garish, all gold and light and water. The promise was subliminal, projections of images and sounds imprinted on me over a lifetime, which somehow made it that much stronger. I couldn't pinpoint who had promised it or when. It was my natural inheritance, waiting.

Today, outside her exam room, the hematologist notices me hunched over, a hand steadying my back. She laughs and says, *I think you should go across the street,* meaning to the women's hospital. *Let them check you out. Seems like more than a normal ache to me.* It doesn't take much to convince me. For days I've been on the lookout for signs that labor might be near. What about that twitch waking me in the night? Could that spotting be the infamous "bloody show"? But I was also aware of those omnipresent stories of women jumping the gun—primitive, hormonal excitement overpowering their rational brains, steering them to the hospital with false contractions, only to be turned away and told they had misread their own bodies. Those silly girls, overestimating their pain and its significance. Making a big fuss over nothing!

In the early part of the twentieth century, as hospital birth became de rigueur, a fear spread among some mothers that their babies would be switched by the medical staff, that they would go home and slowly, slowly, as their newborn grew into itself, its emerging eyes and nose and mouth would harden into the features of a stranger. What if, in the chaos of the nursery, down the sanitized hall from the maternity ward, one child got swapped for another? I wonder if I will recognize my baby, if the Trevi fountain magic will mean an instant bolt of recognition when I see it for the first time—*Yes, that is mine.*

For a time, when I lived in another city, I was afraid of hitting a person while driving and not realizing it. I worried I would miss the impact. Back at my apartment, I checked the car for dents. Not so much fear of hitting a person as fear of the fatal error gone unnoticed and the sin I might carry, secret to myself. I knew I had not hit anyone, but knowledge didn't lessen my fear. Anxiety over an unwitting accident persists in the hematology clinic. How could I trust myself again if something critical happened to my own body, and I could only assemble it from the leftover pieces, after the fact? In the car or on the operating table, I would be a protagonist without memory of the crime.

A story I won't tell: How I was afraid of being wrong about my body.

I call Jed from the elevator bank. He tells me he's going to bike over from his office a couple miles south of the hospital. It doesn't take him long to arrive, adrenaline powering his long legs. His height was one of the first things I'd noticed about him, a decade earlier, across a university theater. I was high on my newly-acquired, collegiate sense of capital "A" Adulthood, my friends and I so engaged in culture and what felt to us like deeply important undertakings—campus protests with seemingly national import; research papers we fantasized would revolutionize the field; deep conversations late at night, folk music playing in the background. I didn't understand how young I was, how the adulthood I was trying on was a thin costume, and how much change still sat on the horizon.

That night in the theater, cosseted in my false maturity, I was struck not just by Jed's height but by the way he carried his frame with a steady assurance. He had nothing to prove. I could tell without speaking to him that he wasn't pompous, didn't think himself better than anyone else, but trusted himself completely. I remember watching him bend down to drink from the water fountain in the lobby before our friends introduced us, his neck arching. Now, as he bends down to place the bike into the rack, the arch of his body echoes that memory.

He walks toward me, unable to suppress the smile on his face—so wide it's almost goofy. The decision to have a child was a joint one, but he was the more eager half of our duo, ready before I was, when we could hardly afford our tiny walk-up apartment and groceries for two, waiting for me to catch up to his enthusiasm before we forged ahead.

We stand together on the sidewalk outside the women's hospital, harried doctors and medical students striding past while checking their pagers, delivery trucks beeping as they back into garages. I lean into Jed when the contractions start and he rubs the small of my back. When the pain departs, I take bites from a crushed granola bar he pulls from the recesses of his messenger bag. I was warned in the hospital labor class that, once admitted to the ward, I wouldn't be allowed to eat. Clear liquids only in case of an emergency c-section. Labor, the instructor had said, telling us to eat a protein-rich meal before leaving the house, could be especially long for a first child. I would need my strength.

I watch the doors pulse open and shut, knowing that when we pass through, I'll leave part of myself stranded here on the busy sidewalk: once you leave you can't return. I'm at the peak of a mountain, looking back where I came from, seeing blurry glimpses of the college kid in the theater, and then turning towards the paths snaking down the other side, unfamiliar and obscured.

In a copy of *Natural Childbirth,* a pregnancy and delivery guide published in 1950 that I will find years later in a Little Free Library, I'll read about "Mrs. William Johnson" who, like me, woke with a backache. "Her husband grunted but did not awaken and Mrs. Johnson momentarily debated whether to wake him or not. She felt that labor was starting but, since this was her first pregnancy she could not be sure." So little has changed in the intervening decades. The doubt creeps in for Mrs. Johnson, for me, for so many others—lying in bed, feeling the body but not sure if we're feeling it the right way, if we know how to interpret our own pain. We're suddenly on our own, estranged from the self that existed before and the one who will emerge after.

The doorman in a red vest greets me at the hospital entrance like he does all the women, with the "Happy Birthday" song. It's made him a legend.

Jed grabs my hand, squeezes, and we walk through. His smile doesn't fade.

We check in at triage, a place labeled by process. Here, functionaries rush to dole out degrees of severity like tinned war rations. They place me in a small, cell-like room, gown me in an open-backed robe, attach probes, read tracings, huddle to discuss, report back, load me into a wheelchair, push it down the hall, onto an elevator, down another hall, around one corner, another. Pastels of thatched cottages nestled beside streams and fields and groves—nearly identical—line beige walls. Signs alone indicate location. I'm a parcel shipped to its destination.

For a moment, I worry I've lost Jed in the jumble of movement amongst the scurrying nurses and the cords running from my body to IV poles, the long, winding hallways. But then I hear his footsteps, the long spaces between his strides, a steady reassurance. We turn and turn, traveling far from the singing doorman.

Weeks before, on the back patio of the coffee shop near our apartment, a woman asked me if my name was _____. *I'm looking for someone who's pregnant*, she said, *and thought it might be you.* She continued walking, iced coffee dribbling condensation onto the pavement. It was the first hot day of summer, when no one in Chicago could believe their good fortune. The woman located the right pregnant woman and the pregnant woman's husband and they sat at the table next to mine. The woman was a doula. She introduced her philosophy (birth as natural process guided by the female body's intuition), her role (to guide the couple according to their personalized birth plan), and various packages available for purchase (prenatal massage, accompaniment to a clinic visit, labor attendance, postpartum care, lactation assistance, phone consults). Birth as sacred and pure and transcending the muck of the everyday, and also as customizable combo deal, and finally, as complex, inscrutable entity necessitating professional navigation and strategizing, to the tune of many hundreds of dollars and a library of specialized texts to be studied and meticulously annotated. I listened closely, staring off in the other direction to hide my eavesdropping. This was a chance to gather up clues about what lay ahead. And yet the information was all second-hand—the pregnant woman of course had not yet delivered her baby, and the doula looked young, unlikely to have experienced birth herself. Still, it was better than nothing.

Let's say, proposed the husband, patting his wife's abdomen—which struck me as a gross violation of her personhood, vicious interruption of autonomy couched in a stroke so gentle she didn't flinch—*that her water breaks but there aren't any contractions. How long should we wait at home? Won't the hospital want to induce? We don't want an induction. How can we avoid one? We want this all to be natural.* He swept his hands in an arc encompassing the baby and his wife and much more. A squirrel pounced on the branch above, shaking leaves loose.

That's where I come in. The doula smiled, sensing the perfect entry for her pitch. *Most likely I'd advise you to stay home until absolutely necessary, to see if the contractions pick up on their own and only go in after they're regular and minutes apart. But that's the sort of thing we can consult on if and when it happens. That's exactly what I'm here for.*

This continued: posing of imaginary labor scenario in which x or y veered off course, followed by solution whereby said course is righted. Doctors as necessary annoyances, barriers to be navigated so forces within could take their course unfettered. I swallowed the last grainy sip of my coffee and thought it strange how people wished to exercise control over the uncontrollable, over nature, instilling such meaning into a handful of hours—a fraction of their lives.

The delivery room swallows me—cavernous space, steel arms shooting from crevices in the walls. These walls suck time. It is impossible to track how long since we entered. We're inside a casino, warren of dinging slot machines and gin-soaked carpets and rings of billowing smoke casting film over everything. I could lose myself in this unending labyrinth.

When I was eight or nine, I sang in the chorus of a church production of *Godspell.* I had a terrible voice and couldn't dance but decided being a Broadway star was the best way to live an authentic adult life. I sensed that in this way I could access the full range of emotion and human experience kids were kept cordoned off from. No one had the heart to tell me the truth about my abilities. Progressive parenting dictated that children be allowed to dream. We chorus members dressed in rainbow colors and flung ourselves at Jesus, who wore a Superman T-shirt and a wide grin. He stood at the cross and drooped his head against his chest to signify a last breath. The cast wept. For the final number, we broke into triumphant song and dance. A revel in melodrama.

The play told a tale of transformation, a sort of magic unfolding within a person that defied my understanding. As a Jewish kid in the Deep South I knew about Christianity, but only via Santa Claus and church spires and the ashy foreheads the day after Mardi Gras—the dominant culture against which my family and community sat in sharp relief. I knew nothing of its theology.

Godspell was the first time I encountered the actual story of Christ. A human seamlessly morphed into a god, sadness and despair into abundant joy. The act of staging the play echoed this alchemy; regular people walked onto the altar/stage and converted into characters. I sometimes felt uneasy watching Jesus, a lanky teenager with a long face, his long hair tied back in a low ponytail, as he did ordinary things, like sitting backstage with his feet on a table or chugging from a soda can or hopping out of the car at the door to the church. I wanted to be transformed too, but it was so hard to let my guard down, as much as I tried, hard to let the music wash over me. I was always aware of myself as an unchanging presence—shy, contained, not wildly-adoring Jesus follower saved by dint of faith—even in a colorful costume and under the bright stage lights.

I lie in the delivery bed under the bright hospital lights and clogs clank into the room. I'm relieved to find my own OB on call today. *What timing!* Dr. G. wears a baggy, oatmeal-colored sweater over her scrubs and it flaps around her. Jed rises from his chair and stands next to me while she pokes inside and examines the bedside screens. He shuffles his feet to make sure he stays out of her way. I can tell from the way he shifts his body in small, incremental movements that he's looking for his place on this strange set. He's part of the action, but also sidelined. He knows he's not the patient, not the main event. He's had no preparation for this, apart from the birthing class where we spent five minutes leaning back into our partners while they practiced applying deep pressure as a "comfort measure," and he has almost certainly spent less time and effort than I have foraging for clues about what to expect. He's seen the diaper commercial births, too, but they haven't ingrained themselves as part of his schema. Satisfied with her checks, Dr. G. leaves me in the nurse's care. Jed retreats back to the recliner in the corner. All is well.

In the hematologist's waiting room one day, a cancer patient seated beside me told me about her son, an addict, and how Jesus had saved him and got her through the ordeal, too. *Don't be too lenient with your child.* She pointed at my stomach, its own character in her drama, though also a part of me.

Around us, elderly men hunched over walkers and scooted from the receptionist's window to the coffee station in the corner where they filled Styrofoam cups with brownish water and powdered creamer; bald, chemo-hollowed women paged through anodyne magazines—*Redbook, Good Housekeeping, Woman's Day.* I felt exempt from the world's random cruelty on full display, my belly safely cordoning me away in the mystical world of expectant motherhood. My body was building up, theirs were breaking down. And yet it was disorienting to be in this place so coated in the suffocating film of illness. The waiting room of my OB's office, by contrast, was medical but safely removed from the realm of illness and injury and impending mortality—populated by well-coiffed young women clutching their newly printed ultrasound photos, strutting around with their stomachs proudly wrapped in spandex. These mothers-to-be had the same falsely earned confidence of college-student me, stepping into the garments of the next stage before knowing what it entailed. I probably did, too.

A nurse called the mother of the Christ-saved child back for her appointment. She rose and waved to me and also to the thing becoming a child inside me— a warning wave so I wouldn't forget her advice. The automatic door shut behind her and I imagined the Jesus of *Godspell* diving down to fish her son out of the depths of some murky lake. The lanky actor emerging onto the muddy banks with the gasping, sputtering sinner draped over his muscled arms, shaking his wild mane out, splashing water back and forth like a holy Baywatch lifeguard.

I stayed there in the waiting room, anticipating my own metamorphosis. Now I was *woman*, soon I would be *mother*, which I had been told was something other than mere woman. It would change everything about me, including my writing, a professor had told me when I announced my pregnancy; it would make me attuned to the smallest things I now overlooked. *Mother* I couldn't yet comprehend, but I would know it when it arrived. I could foresee the brilliant metaphors and images raining down on me as I changed explosive diapers and wiped drool, the sacred and profane colliding.

We wait. When Dr. G. returns, she looks at me, at the monitor, at me again. The nurse sidles up to her, ready to help. Something has been communicated without words. The nurse knows she's needed. *Okay, I'm going to break your water,* Dr. G. notifies us. *Speed up those contractions.*

Ok! I agree, enthusiastic about anything that will move us closer to meeting the baby, to that revelatory, gleaming moment the whole pregnancy has been leading up to. I've seen water breaking in movies before—a sudden, sometimes hilarious, balloon-pop of clear fluid announcing what's to come. Finally I'm back to being part of a show, a la *Godspell*.

Jed is suddenly next to me. I didn't see him rise from the chair; he evaporated and reappeared. *Ok*, he says, trying not to get lost in the shuffle. I'm glad for his voice, his ceremonial seal of approval—a reminder that I'm not completely alone on the soundstage. He's in the ensemble.

The doctor rolls up the sleeves of her sweater, gloves her hands, prods me with a long, thin tool. *Just like a crochet hook,* she says, as if that incantation will line the sterile white walls with tapestry, carpet linoleum floors in plush, transport me to some oversized armchair warmed by roaring fire.

From inside, greenish-black sludge oozes. Nothing like the clear fluid of the movies. The set seems to darken around me. *Thick mec,* Dr. G. says; the alchemy she performed has gone slightly awry. What would the doula have had to say about this scenario? Jed places a hand on my back as the course instructor advised but I push him aside and crouch down. This isn't normal pain and it's suddenly ridiculous that a bit of pressure might relieve it. I've never experienced anything of this magnitude. In fact it's so strong it's not really pain anymore, but I have no other words to label it.

Breaking the water has opened the dam of contractions. At the start of each, I can't see how I'm going to make it to the end without splitting down the middle; somehow, though, I stay in one piece, begin to breathe as it relents, and then, before I know it there's another, and another.

Dr. Grantly Dick-Read's 1942 treatise on natural labor, *Childbirth Without Fear,* proclaims pain is simply a physical manifestation of errant thought. Change the mind and click, pain dissipates. He instructs with fervor, with the confidence of one who has himself squatted on all fours to allow a baby's descent through the birth canal. Fear untamed, he warns, digs in with almost literal claws; he describes a case in which extreme fright, translated into muscle tension, constricts and cinches, eventually draining the uterus of blood until it glows white.

Both *Childbirth Without Fear* and the book from the Little Free Library harken back to a halcyon era of pure birth, natural birth unimpeded by the march of modernity—the paleo diet of labor and delivery. That it never really existed doesn't matter. These men happily elide that childbirth meant death for many, for as long as there have been humans, heads too large to slip effortlessly through the pelvis. Their books argue that if women simply try hard enough, if they are woman enough, they might find empowerment in the pain. They might even find the pain transformed into something that is not pain and that could bring with it spiritual transcendence. This, after all, was what female bodies were made for, their biological destiny, an almost Aristotelian fulfillment. For a fleeting moment in the throes of agony properly channeled, the woman could become the ideal version of herself, not just *a* woman but *The Woman*. What would these doctors have done if they'd glimpsed the future: the many pregnant people today throwing off the yoke of rigid gender norms, some of whom are not women at all, who approach birth without any thought of fulfilling so-called biological destiny, chafing against the notion? Would Dr. Grantly-Read and his associates have sat dumbfounded and watched, open-mouthed and wide-eyed, as the whole edifice they'd constructed caved in on itself? Or would they have dug in their heels, clearing their throats and shouting their theories at the masses like white-coated, British-accented versions of internet trolls?

Water breaking isn't an event that ends. Once it breaks, it keeps going. They don't show that part in movies either.

I like to believe I'm the sort of person who screams for an epidural, but decorum gets the better of me. I ask. Wait. Maybe I'm afraid of what it means to fall short of the sort of womanhood outlined by those male authors. Maybe I don't trust the depth of my pain. I climb onto an exercise ball. *It helps distribute pressure*, the nurses say. I think balancing on a curved, slippery surface simply distracts as contractions expel me from my skin, relent, allow me back. Jed stands beside me, trying to reassure with his presence but not confident he can help after I've rebuffed his previous efforts.

In the Victorian era, pain in childbirth posed a Catch-22. If a woman failed to experience sufficient pain, men deemed her overly bold, deficient in femininity. Yet admitting too much pain rendered her weak, hardly up to the virtuous tasks of motherhood and household management. Always either too much woman or too little—to say nothing of Black women, who doctors once argued were naturally less susceptible to pain than white women, and, by extension, less womanly. This dangerous myth lingers, in spite of attempts to expunge it; hospitals still discount the pain of black women, too often ignoring their symptoms until the damage is done.

Today the obsession with pain and how to feel it persists. There are birthing classes advising women on how to thread the needle and achieve that longed-for balance, the just-right amount of pain, but here on the ball in the delivery room I can see that the tips were all platitudes, tricking us unsuspecting women into thinking we could choose the perfect path, that we had any control. There may be more options than there once were, but we're still essentially working from the Victorian assumption that the way we manage our bodies dictates our future as mothers. Are you an epidural mother or a natural mother? Are you the kind of person who wants to feel your baby come into the world or would you rather be numb?

When I'm mid-contraction, the anesthesiologist finally strolls in. He hardly seems to notice I can't catch my breath or actually register my existence at all. I'm a patient to him, not a full person. He speaks of me, not to me, instructing the nurses to help me move from the ball back onto the bed, edge me to the lip of the mattress. He points Jed to the door and orders him to leave to create a sterile field. Jed gives me a look on his way out as though acknowledging my existence as more than mere medical specimen. The door clicks shut after him.

Don't move a muscle, the anesthesiologist warns, hovering his needle over me. I can't see the sharp point but I can almost feel it, a tautness in the air behind me, a threat. *Still*, the anesthesiologist barks. Apparently I have moved. This is why doctors refuse to administer epidurals in the late stages of labor; the contractions come on too fast and too strong. I'm not that far into labor, only four centimeters dilated, Dr. G. told me, before she broke my water, and already it's nearly impossible to control my movements. A jolt could cause the needle to puncture the wrong spot on the spine, which, for obvious reasons, could have devastating consequences. I hunch, hold my breath, organs ricocheting, my back an exposed bent arc swiped clean with singe of alcohol. I clench my fists, jaw, feet.

The cold concoction settles in and my skin fills with the soggy weight of numbness. I am someone altered. I look for Jed through the vertical patch of window in the door, but I can't see him.

The word *epidural* is an adjective shoehorned into a noun. In its purest form it describes the space surrounding the dura mater, that *dense, tough outermost membranous envelope of the brain and spinal cord*—emphasis on texture, on impenetrability. The womb has the same cloak of opacity. There are only indirect methods for determining what it contains. You can't exactly peer inside. Unlike the delivery room door with its small rectangle of glass, there's no uterine window (the secrecy an evolutionary adaptation, I am told, to cocoon the fetus away from danger). So much of pregnancy and birth is about trying to see through a body intent on concealing itself: a due date is a guess based on averages; doctors can only extrapolate from sound waves to determine fetal size; perinatal researchers float untested hypotheses about cause and effect, creating a stack of off-limits food and medication and activities that may be fine but also may not be—no one knows, and so better safe than sorry. Being pregnant can feel like a transformation into a precious China doll protected in a case, and then labor hits and the doll gets taken out, thrown on the floor, smashed to pieces over and over again.

Now that my pain is gone, or at least shoved underground, I call my friend and ask her to stop at our apartment and bring our "go bag"— vocabulary absorbed from birthing class where they instructed us on what to pack—and camera. Weeks ago I diligently filled a suitcase with the recommended accoutrements: socks and ChapStick for those labor-parched lips, face wash and a cotton robe marketed specifically to nursing mothers though identical to any other cotton robe, the cutest baby outfit and blanket we had. Like packing for a weekend trip to some strange resort.

We can get it later, Jed says. The nurse has let him slip back into the room, and he sits on his perch, a chair pulled up to the bedside, relieved and perhaps a little surprised at my sudden calm.

No, I tell him, *we need the camera. We have to take a picture right away.*

He nods. He knows better than to argue. I can do nothing—I'm numb below the waist, confined to this narrow bed and weighed down by IV needles in my arms and monitors strapped across my belly. At least I can decide this.

Already I know what photos we'll take: me half-reclined, sloshed in a cocktail of wild exhaustion and elation, skin dewy, bun messy, hospital gown falling off my shoulder's edge as I hold a faceless, ruddy baby; me and Jed and said faceless baby huddled together, stitched to each other in our new identity as family, all three on the edge of delirium (the nurse will take this one, of course, hurriedly, between medical tasks, and the angle would be slightly off, the light from the window washing out our faces, but the imperfection will be part of the aesthetic).

Later I will show the faceless baby these pictures as evidence of the miraculous event, the moment it made me a mother. *Look,* I'll say. *You arrived and I was never the same.* I'll also show them to the audience as I narrate the birth story I think I'll tell, the one that begins with the car ride to the routine appointment—*little did I know.*

A few weeks before my due date, we bought a kitchen table from a couple with a three-month-old who slept soundly in a swing by the fireplace. *You should have a natural birth,* the mother advised when she saw me. I knew only her first name, her email, and her address, and yet she threw this out as though we were deeply enmeshed. Her unwashed hair swept down over one of her puffy eyes like a shield. *It's miraculous,* she told me, *though to be honest I still have nightmares about the pain. They wake me up.* She fumbled with her necklace, something large and glittering. Maybe a push present, I thought. That was a concept I liked to poke fun at with Jed, the notion that a woman should get a jewel for labor, that she needed to be rewarded for a natural thing. It felt so transactional, so capitalist. In trying to assign value to motherhood it undercut the whole project. But I hadn't yet undergone birth, had no nightmares from the pain, so what did I know?

Wow, I said back to her, which sounded like the exact wrong reply as soon as it came out.

Yeah. She nodded. *But still, I can't imagine not feeling that crucial moment,* she continued, in a rush to explain. *It's a physical bond I'll always have my baby.*

Suddenly alarms begin to beep. Lines flit and dive across the screen. Nurses come to the bedside. They turn me one way, then, when *Baby doesn't like that,* another. Secure an oxygen mask over my nose and mouth, peel it off. Record my blood pressure and temperature and feed me ice chips from a pink bucket.

I have four nurses in total—a stack of cards, shuffled and reshuffled. One comes in, erases the old name on the whiteboard across from the bed, writes the new. Two in the first shift—one in training, one senior—then one confused by everything, who mispronounces Dr. G.'s name and is quietly removed and replaced. The last one has a plain face and a plainer name and is kind and competent in a way that matches her plainness. She stays for the duration.

When the chaos subsides, the delivery room feels strangely vast: plenty of space for huddles of doctors and nurses and unfurling equipment. Without the force of my contractions, I am untethered in it, suspended.

In the dim studio light, the yoga instructor tested us. *Can you tell the difference between good pain and bad?* She wanted us to embrace the discomfort of a deep stretch but not go so far as to pull a muscle or otherwise injure ourselves. She didn't gesture toward pain that can't be felt, damage that takes place in numbness, perhaps the most dangerous kind.

Every hour Dr. G. clanks in, checks the width of my cervix and the positioning of the baby's head in the birth canal, ensuring all is progressing according to protocol.

When she leaves, only Jed, alternating between his chair and my bedside, the nurse who matches the name on the board, and I remain within grasp of the room's arms.

You're doing a great job, Jed says. He stands beside me, his body reflected in the darkening windows, confident and sure of his pronouncement. But I'm not doing anything. Processes are happening to me, doctors and nurses are inserting things into me and adjusting things around me.

Outside of this room, in the other delivery rooms on the floor, I know people are walking and talking and grunting and screaming. But I can't hear any of it from within these soundproofed walls. We're an ecosystem, the three of us, and also the machines captioning the movements inside me and the baby contained beneath.

They don't tell you, I say to the plain nurse, *that labor is really just waiting.*

I know, she says. *Almost boring, isn't it?*

In her Victorian-era manual for birth, *Preparation for Motherhood,* Elisabeth Robinson Scovil writes: "The word pelvis is derived from a Greek term meaning a dish or bowl. It is the bony basin forming the lower part of the body. The hip bones are the highest point on each side. From these it slopes down until in front there is only a comparatively narrow rim called the pubic arch. The side of the bowl below this is cut away, and it is under this arch that the child passes at the time of birth." The Victorians like to anesthetize the body with the language of a porcelain catalog—cultured people describing the qualities of dishware rather than the rawness of skin and sinew. Scovil doesn't mention the China doll thrown down on the floor and broken into pieces.

I want to know: Is time a bowl or a plate? Are the sides sloped so some things happen faster than others, a sort of exponential curve? Or flat and even—constant? Or both: sometimes one thing and sometimes another?

I'm not sure what has altered the flow of time since our arrival at the hospital. There are so many factors: winding hallways and the torrent of personnel in and out and the epidural's numbing. Or, it might be a quality endemic to the pummeling of the baby from my body. In order to churn out another person, a woman has to transform into something not quite human. It certainly isn't anything out of a porcelain catalog. It's not subhuman, and it also isn't godly. There's nothing sacred going on here. But when the body gets pushed aside, so, it turns out, are the laws of physics. I may as well have lived my whole life in this bed, cordoned off from the world, time sloshing through. Nothing has prepared me for this, not the books I read or the class I took downstairs from this very room or the eavesdropped conversations at the coffee shop.

Again the alarms go off and Dr. G. rushes in. Jed backs away to give her space. She says she may wheel me to the OR because of a pattern on the monitors. *All right,* I say, *but will I be put under for surgery?* She's been working with the hematologist to manage my disappearing platelets, which, if below a certain threshold, make certain kinds of anesthesia too risky. *You could bleed out on the table,* Dr. G. cautioned, before, in her windowless exam room. But that seemed far-fetched. What woman in the modern world bleeds to death giving birth in a first-rate teaching hospital occupying prime lakefront real estate?

The idea of surgery doesn't scare me, but being asleep during birth still does. I don't want to become one of those women from the early days of hospital births, examining their babies, brought in from a bath in the nursery, for signs of kinship.

Nope, Dr. G. comforts, gloving her hands. The latex snaps: one, two. *We've already got the epidural in place. For a section we just add an extra dose of medication to numb you completely. But,* she adds, *before we jump to surgery, let's see if Baby responds to stimulation.* She pulls herself closer. *I'm going to tickle Baby's head.* She reaches inside, staring at the screen as she prods. I am part machine/part other being/part self; a cord runs from the monitor inside me where a probe sticks to the fetal head. I feel nothing. *All good!* she declares. The heart rate has apparently stabilized. *And,* she adds, *Baby has a full head of hair!* How strange that the head is right there, but hidden. Close enough to some revelation that we can feel its texture.

Our families text Jed: *any updates??*

What should I say? he asks, showing me the phone. He doesn't want to speak for me.

Tell them there's not much to report, I say. *Tell them we're just waiting.*

You can rest now, the nurse says. It's the middle of the night. *Try to sleep. There's nothing else to do while we wait.*

Hours pass and I can't sleep. Jed manages to doze off on the pull-out a few times and I wake him out of boredom and anticipation and an indignant sense that it isn't right for him to rest when I can't. He rubs his eyes to try to keep himself alert. I feel selfish for wanting him awake, but then I remember what's happening to me, even if I can't feel it: my body cranking itself open. It's pitch-black outside but for the glow of streetlights below. I'll have one of those babies born in the early morning hours. These are the hours best suited for birth, hidden away from the architecture of the everyday. Nighttime is another feature embedded in the birthing blueprint I've been handed: waking in the night to the thud of contractions, rushing to the hospital on empty streets. Sun would mess the whole thing up.

Ten centimeters, Dr. G. announces triumphantly. She's back in the room. She means I'm fully dilated, that my body has released enough oxytocin to cause my uterus to shudder and squeeze my baby's head down, drill against cervix, so it opens wide enough to expel the infant. The complex mechanics of an organic Rube Goldberg machine.

Jed rises, his eyes suddenly wide open and alert. He dusts his hands on the thighs of his jeans, ready to jump the threshold into parenthood. I'm still lying flat in the bed, feet stirruped.

Dr. G. tells us she will call a pediatric team into the room for delivery because of the thick meconium-stained liquor from the water breaking that never ends. Liquor. It sounds luxurious, velvet, baby swaddled in moonshine, opaque and rich and dizzying, instead of what I know meconium to be—an infant's first bowel movement, sticky and putrid and green.

It's our protocol, she explains, detaching the delivery bed bottom in preparation for the end. *So Baby doesn't aspirate the mec into the lungs. You won't be able to hold Baby at first,* she says. *They'll need to suction the liquor so it isn't inhaled deep into the lungs.*

Mec is short for meconium, but no one bothers to translate. Dr. G. fumbles inside one of the bins brimming with metal tools. *Baby won't cry right away. In fact, we don't want Baby to cry until suctioning is complete and the mec cleared from its airway. It will only take a minute but that minute will seem like an eternity*, she warns.

Ok, I say.

Ok, Jed says.

Do not be alarmed, she says. *After they're done, the pediatricians will hand Baby back over to you.* She enters something into the computer. *Do not be alarmed.*

Baby, the medical staff all say, lopping off the article. It's simply *Baby. Baby seems more comfortable in this position. Baby is in no hurry to get out. Baby is giving us a run for our money.* The hospital morphs *baby* into a proper noun and, in doing so, quasi-anthropomorphizes it—human, sure, but on the cusp. Its stance towards the parents is strangely infantilizing, echoing the way a preschool teacher speaks to her charges. As though the mother (or *Mama*, as the staff like to call me, and I presume other laboring women) needs things fed to her, bite-sized and deposited directly in her mouth.

Prepare ye the way of the Lord, goes the opening song of *Godspell*. And that's it. *Prepare ye the way of the Lord. Prepare ye the way of the Lord. Prepare ye the way of the Lord.* The chorus jumped side to side and waved their hands overhead. I'd never before felt so much a part of something. The me faded into the collective.

I push for two hours, but it might be two minutes or two days. I'm a factory worker in charge of a switch. The final nurse, plain face and plain name, studies a tracing of my contractions and tells me when to bear down, when to ease up.

1,2,3, go, she chants.

She knows more of my body than I do. The anesthesiologist returns and lowers the epidural dose so I can feel something (pressure, not pain, he is careful to distinguish, like those male doctors of history, with curious insight into the birthing body). It's important that I am able to sense my muscles squeeze the baby so I can use this feeling to propel and amplify my efforts. Jed stands next to me, side-lined; he cannot read the monitors and cannot feel the tightening. I know I push for two hours because Dr. G. says, *I'll let you push for two hours, but that's the limit*—like I've begged for time and we've reached this deal after tense, drawn-out negotiation. *Baby can't han-dle too much*, she says, *of the pushing*. I don't know what this means but there is a lot I don't understand. More than I can ask about while my body heaves.

So that I could better understand the plot of *Godspell,* my mom bought me a book about Jesus at The Catholic Bookstore, a con-verted bungalow situated on an oak-lined avenue. I knew under-standing was important to acting. An actor had to turn part of him-self into the character in order to convince the audience, and this was only possible with knowledge.

From the book I learned real Jesus was human, born to a woman in a manger, but also god. Similarly, his death was preordained and necessary for salvation, but also mourned. The contradictions didn't bother me. Childhood might be defined as the state of holding many truths at once. Aging occurs when that simultaneity breaks down and we must pick one or the other.

Pregnancy is another sort of breaking down, taking the self apart to create another. Puking into the toilet in my first trimester, I felt the detritus left behind from that cleaving exit my body. I felt it flowing up my throat, through my lips. I was purging the mess out to make room for what was next.

Between pushes, the nurse slips the soaked green sheet out from under me, slaps down a clean one. Single fluid motion, easy to miss.

1, 2, 3, go.

Somewhere out of sight—hidden from monitors and hovering nurses and Jed and me—a tightening. A narrowing. Almost pastoral, rapids slow to a serene trickle over moss-covered rocks. The flow restricts and, for a moment, time grinds to a halt. Here in the delivery room, the blood pressure cuff squeezes my arm every few minutes. After a while I barely register the compression. When it's done, the cuff releases with an audible sigh.

I was not a nester—one of those pregnant women who delight in placing chevron decals in rows along the nursery walls and stacking baby blankets just so in the closet. Perhaps this was the result of absorbing lingering Jewish superstition: babies aren't a thing to be counted on until birth. Or maybe it pointed to insufficient investment in this internal creature who I didn't believe would become my baby until I held it and it cried.

Instead of nesting, I broke down in the aisle of the baby store. How could they name the store something as crass as BuyBuy Baby? I wanted to know. There were too many gliders to choose from and they all cost too much. I couldn't' figure out if I was offended by the materialism or overwhelmed by my inability to navigate the storm of supplies.

We don't need any of this stuff, Jed argued. But I was less convinced. On the shelves: special scarves for breastfeeding privacy, specialty nail clippers that wouldn't fissure skin, pulse ox monitors with cutesy names designed to detect danger in the night, bottles with inserts to ease digestion, fitted car seat covers for snow and rain and shades for summer and swaddle blankets made out of muslin and cotton and fleece to keep babies at exactly the right temperature. Every item facilitating a happy, healthy baby. We couldn't buy it all even if we wanted to, not on a grad student and law clerk budget. Besides, we didn't need it all. If only I knew how to distinguish between needed and not.

I couldn't see then that I was not so different from the couple interviewing the doula in the coffee shop, dragged into the crass commercialization of birth and parenthood as a means to control the uncontrollable. Without realizing it, I'd bought into the hype. I saw the images of the happy babies smiling at their tired, happy moms (or well-rested actors pretending to be tired, happy moms) on the boxes of video monitors promising that I could watch my infant on a static-free screen as I luxuriated in the comfort of my own bed. Even as I bucked against the idea that I needed an expensive tool to provide postpartum bliss, I couldn't help but see my future self in that model mother, open arms awaiting my future baby brought out from the hidden crevice of the womb. At the OB's, I trusted the various blood tests and ultrasounds that indicated a healthy baby and didn't think about the fact that there were hundreds or thousands of conditions sitting outside the purview of these diagnostics. All of it—the Nose Frida contraption straight out of more evolved Scandinavia and promising efficient snot removal from a congested infant, and the clear first-trimester screen designed to detect genetic diseases—affirming my naïve assumption that progress and technology had gotten women to a place of perfection. We don't die in childbirth anymore, I thought, imagining with a shudder what it would be like to approach one's due date like a coin toss that would determine life or death. Now babies arrive healthy—rosy and rooting. I assumed we'd moved above and beyond, outside of risk and danger, ascended to a higher plane. In my cocoon, perhaps aided and abetted by the fact of my whiteness, I conveniently ignored how recently history had removed women from this grave threat, and how the danger still, sometimes, lurked.

Okay, Dr. G. says. My two hours are up, alarm gone off. She removes her oatmeal-colored sweater to reveal green scrubs, holds up bright silver forceps. *Imagine sterile salad tongs,* she says, as though alluding to the crochet hook she used to break my water. But the water didn't come out clear as I was promised by the movies, and this new instrument is too strange and medieval for domestic metaphor. Some of the room's arms emerge from the walls and ceiling. Lights brighten. More doctors and nurses converge as if they'd been crouched, hiding alongside the arms the whole time. *This is the pediatric team,* Dr G. says, pointing in one direction. *And here is anesthesiology. And there are the OB residents and fellows and nurses.* I don't care about introductions. Too many faces to track. Some wait on the periphery like a chorus; others crowd in, closer. *One last push,* the doctor says. Jed tightens his grip on my hand. For an instant, all I smell is his almost-worn-off Old Spice instead of the cold astringency of the hospital. I'm back home, in bed next to him in our apartment.

Physician Peter Chamberlen developed forceps in the seventeenth century, when doctors began to encroach on the work of midwives, stomping their way into the most feminine of domains. Chamberlen's forceps were novel because they did not necessarily kill the fetus. Until then, tools for delivery, sometimes cooking implements snatched from kitchen drawers, cleaved the baby—impossible to save both mother and child. After all this time sharing one body, their lives were at odds. Hooks tore off limbs and devices pierced skulls and extracted brains. Sometimes, one hopes, the baby died before this dismantling. If the fetus was to be saved over the mother, if she was too far gone, then the baby would be delivered by cesarean section instead; women weren't expected to survive the procedure. In old sketches of the varieties of forceps, they resemble rabbits with large ears.

Let go, the yoga instructor demanded, as we released our bodies into child's pose, hands stretched out on the mat. Here, in the delivery room, I'm ready to let go, if only my body will let me.

1, 2, 3, go the nurse chants as the line of my contraction rises on the screen and her hands rise with it and I take in a deep breath until it throbs all over my body not from the contraction which is faded and worn and more ghost than muscle but from holding it all in and the prongs are deep inside pulling pulling pulling and then the counting is at *8, 9,* and I only hear parts of things because we are all shimmering like breath in cold air and the nurse says *let go* and when I do my neck merges with my arms my eyes with my knees my liver with my heart my stomach with the metal inside nothing solid nothing distinct I might lose myself over the edge and I don't know if I do it or if forceps finish the work.

Jed says: *Its head is a funny shape. It's strange looking. Not like a baby.* He inches away from it. Is it over?

I am not in the bed. A body lies on the bed. I am not contained in the body. I must be stuck in the vent above the room, looking down. I do not know how I got there: shrunken, hiding. Things happen to a body that, at some point, was mine, but I am not part of what happens to it. *I'm stitching you up*, the doctor says to the body. The body can hear the words but cannot understand them. *Your tear isn't too bad for a forceps delivery.* Tear? What tear?

What about the placenta? I ask from above. I remember this part from the hospital's labor and delivery class; it's not over once the baby emerges. Also, from a TV show where a chunk of the ruby red temporary organ sticks to a woman's insides, bleeds, until a midwife reaches her arm up and up, a plumber's auger, and dislodges the stubborn part.

Already out, the doctor says. The body feels a faint tug. From the vent I see edges of things: feet shuffling, lights brightening, carts wheeling, tubes and wires stretching. They should make noise but don't. It's strangely quiet. Not silent but someone has turned the volume down to 2 or 3 out of 100. I strain to hear.

What's happening? I ask Jed.

Here is what I know:

A baby is born.

The baby is born.

Baby is born.

My baby is born, only Baby is not my baby.

Baby is born, but not completely.

I lie in the bed and Baby is pulled out of me.

I am in the vent when Baby is pulled out of me.

I have nothing to do with Baby's birth.

I am a prop facilitating birth of Baby.

The baby is a baby of the hospital.

I am not the mother.

I am the mother, but I am not there when Baby is born.

Months from now, over takeout Chinese, I will learn that the word "obstetrics" originates from the Latin *obstetricus,* which denotes a midwife. This in turn derives from the root *obstare,* to stand across, as in the position of a midwife vis à vis her patient, and also evokes physical obstacle, something that must be surmounted, gotten around. Confusing because it can't be the midwife who's the obstacle, though she stands across. The midwife coaxes the baby out, doesn't keep it in. Rather it's the woman's body—birth canal, hips, uterus's refusal to contract at appropriate intervals or with enough strength to force open her cervix, elastic gateway from body to world, somehow the cap of the uterus and its own organ—that forms the blockade. The body serves as barrier and pathway, designed to keep its charge inside many months and release it at precisely the right moment, requiring perfect calibration.

The word obstetrics is a trap; the t's press against each other. Perhaps it would sound better if this mealtime internet search and discussion had happened before the events in question, an unheeded warning or literary foreshadowing. If I had been warned that my body was a trap. It did not. If it had, I'm not sure I would have heard it over the jet-engine roar of *What to Expect When You're Expecting* and Babycenter.com advice and the doula's echoing voice and the ads at BuyBuy Baby.

Early in pregnancy, when, according to my book, the baby was the size of a raspberry or blueberry and I was pale with nausea, I walked through my day buoyed, carrying a secret half divine and half mundane. Already I wasn't quite myself, though I might have looked it to the rest of the world. Something elemental had fissured, waiting to be spun out. Everyone gets here by way of a woman carrying a secret, yet I felt like the only one to ever experience this splitting of self. Early pregnancy is a state of suspension between the known, rational world, and the spiritual, irrational, even false. Birth, it turns out, too.

But I'm far from prepared for the total severance I'm now experiencing. The forceps have spliced me into body and specter, watching the action from the ceiling above the bed. I knew that, years ago, childbearing meant confronting the possibility of dying during birth, but I didn't think I'd brush up against that past, not in this state-of-the-art hospital. None of the baby books spoke of what to do if it did. None of the products in the store could help with this kind of time travel.

The thing happening in the delivery room doesn't exist because I don't have words to describe it. This isn't the transition from woman to motherhood I expected. I'm becoming something else, but I don't know what that is. Without language to label it, I can't fathom it. I hadn't foreseen this version of birth—didn't know it was a thing that could happen. Or I knew it could happen, but only in a world and time far from mine, to people who bear little resemblance—faces aged paint on canvas. The ridges of their grief ironed into something remote and historical and featureless.

I remember the day the fissuring began, or at least the day I became aware of it. I peed and the strip pinkened, one of those life clichés, and afterwards I took a long bike ride with Jed and worried that each bump might dislodge the embryo. *No, of course it won't,* Jed said patiently. He reassured me that the kind of splitting I feared wasn't that easy. That I couldn't cause it by accident. But he didn't know.

The fissuring sped with each rapid-fire cell division—the creature, according to my app, morphing from blueberry to raspberry to apple to melon, from embryo to fetus—and now, here, finished with the thing, I'm emptied out and floating in the vent and the fissuring has reached a fever pitch and shows no signs of slowing. I'm splitting faster and faster, breaking down into something I don't recognize, something older, some other past version of myself, spinning backward, inchoate.

Wild West

I keep splitting. The part of me in the bed grips the rails as I spin backwards.

Jackie Kennedy had a miscarriage and then a stillbirth and then a premature baby who died at one day old.

Henry XIII's third wife, Jane Seymour—following Anne Boleyn and her three miscarriages and subsequent trial and beheading—died days after childbirth. Her child survived and, for a short while, reigned as king. Only Jane, of all of Henry's wives, endured unblemished in his mind. Death in childbirth cemented her place as martyr.

In the Bible, women often conceive and bear children in a single sentence. Rachel, wife of Jacob, died giving birth to Benjamin. Joseph, her firstborn: cemented as Jacob's favorite because he resembled his dead mother.

Somewhere a cavewoman without a name gave birth to a son blue and not breathing, buried him in a field.

In a railroad town out west crisscrossed by covered wagons lurching over dirt roads, host to a rat-infested brothel poised above a saloon, I crouch in the squalid outhouse during early labor pains, thinking them indigestion, then realizing no—this is what I've been waiting for.

The pains arrive like the faraway ocean waves I yearn for in this arid landscape: cresting into frantic foam, receding until they meld into the dark quiet glittering far beyond the shore, churning, this time with more speed, cresting again. I retch, doubled over, my face just above the hole in the ground swarming with flies.

Months ago, first with child but still flat and quiet in the belly, I doubted my body in the same way, assumed I'd gotten my dates wrong. But as weeks passed, I could ignore the absence no longer. I felt the change in strange parts: A tingling in the tips of my toes and fingers, a churn in my stomach, a slight ache in the small of my back. I was being inhabited.

I waited to tell my family back East until I felt the quickening—first subtle, a pulse of liquid, organs shifting and settling, then sharp juts and turns, the movements unmistakably of some foreign creature, in me but not of me. *I share happy tidings*, I wrote. *I am with child, expecting this summer. The midwife tells me July, should all continue to be well. I have known now for some months but waited for more certainty before writing.*

Their replies were spare and cautious. They prayed for health and courage and for the birth of a hearty child. They said they would await news and to send a telegram once it had arrived.

While I hunch in the outhouse, I count the days since the midwife visited. Four, no five days ago I laid atop the bed and she spanned her fingers across the center of my abdomen, yanked up my skirts, clicked her tongue against teeth, schoolmarm's note of disapproval though I didn't know what I had done wrong. *Babe's snug in there, but you're nearing the time. Not much more room left here. I give you three more weeks,* she proclaimed, *or thereabouts.* As the preacher's wife, she spoke with his same sermon-like elocution, the voice of a self-made prophet foretelling some vague future while also passing moral judgment on each woman under her care. I could tell I wasn't clean enough or robust enough or modest enough for her liking.

As I sat up and pulled my skirts back down, she placed a small paper package on the table tied with twine. *Raspberry leaves,* she said, patting the sack. *To brew in case the waters spill and the pains don't follow.* She did not believe in the ability of my body. *Some women need encouragement.* She edged away from the bed, eyes downcast. Was there something she was afraid of, a contaminant that might transfer from me to her if she were to look at me directly? The door slammed behind her in the strong frontier wind.

Now the outhouse door bangs open and shut in the same wind. It tumbles over the hills and through the valley where scores of settlers have built their homes. My feet sink into the muddy ground, wet soaking through my leather boots and sweat pooling under my arms and behind my knees. A pain hits, radiating from my center. Each wave builds to something stronger than the one before. As the feeling slides down towards my feet all thought flees my mind. I become blankness, a sieve. It releases and I fill back up again, but I have changed in the interval. What returns isn't quite the same as what left.

I look out of a broken slat and glimpse the outline of my husband through the cabin window. He sits at the fire, something protruding from his lips, perhaps a cigar, his one vice. *Everyone needs something,* he likes to say, squeezing my thigh. *Except you.* But he knows I have mine, too.

I cannot allow him to see me in this degraded state, so returning home is no option. Each night I clean the festering green wound on his elbow where, once, a stray bullet ricocheted against the wall of the general store and dislodged the edge of his bone, necessitating an extraction at the doctor's, weeks of poultices and replacing pus-soaked dressings; but when I bleed each month, I am careful to replace the rags far from his view. If the flow is heavy, I sleep on a bundle of rags by the fire in case blood leaches out. Some of the body—some of nature—is acceptable, some not. This is what must be concealed.

In town, the preacher likes to stand on street corners and speak of Eve's great sin trapping us here in the world of folly: the tree, the fruit, the serpent, woman's primal weakness and temptation and fall, the covering of her shameful nakedness, expulsion, and, finally, the pains of labor inflicted upon her that make her feel she might die, and sometimes do indeed smite her. It's woman's curse to carry, that birth should hew so closely to death, and from it follows the unspoken rule that babies may be seen cloaked under the mother's skirts while still inside, and once they are born, but not during the transition between realms. From this, men must be shielded.

Down beside the putrid hole in the ground, I am too tired from the cresting pains to think of where else I might go. With each tightening, my insides barrel down to the base of my pelvis.

I am not sure if I sleep here in the mud or if I am caught in a perpetual state of waiting and tightening, my body led up to the verge of breaking, then retreating from the edge.

Here, in the thick, still heat, shit festers and clogs air.

Morning comes, and I gather my strength and hobble towards the preacher's cabin, the midwife's home. The preacher, I hope, is away pacing the muddy streets of town, ministering to what he calls the lost souls. *Here we are, sinners wandering through the wilderness like the Israelites in the desert. In time we will christen this sacred land, anoint it with God's word!* he shouts. He knows—we all know—it is only the wayward who seek out a life in this desolate, wild place where they think they can bend the land to their will.

I rap my mud-crusted knuckles at the door. Wait. An animal skitters in the brush. I knock again. A child calls for his mother. Finally, the midwife answers. Her plain eyes set within her plain, pitted face look me up and down. She takes the shawl from her shoulders and wraps it around me. This is when I realize the completeness of my sorry state, how fully the pains have overtaken me, because she is not a woman to readily lend what is hers. She's a Christian, of course, though not a particularly charitable one. Probably I smell of piss and shit, though a person mercifully grows accustomed to their own odor.

Shoo, the midwife says to her children, as though hustling away a litter of stray cats. *Shoo.*

The older children scuttle out first, sidling against the wall, careful not to touch me. They steal pitying glances back in my direction. One holds his nose. After the straggling toddler fetches her rag doll and disappears outside with the others, the midwife turns to me, wiping her hands on her calico apron, obscuring knots of flowers in a dust of white. *I didn't expect to see you here so soon,* she scolds, guiding me into the center of the room. Her voice holds disappointment, that I chose to come earlier than she deemed appropriate, that I didn't fend off the pains for a few more days or weeks. She closes the door. The place quiets.

I can't help but think of my husband. Is he worried for me? Does he realize where I have disappeared to? I hope he has some premonition of what is occurring. He is a man who protects, and there is plenty in this place that demands protection—but also plenty beyond his grasp.

The midwife pushes corn husks off the table, spreads out a layer of old newspaper, gestures for me to climb up. *So I can look you over,* she says, tilting her head towards the table. She taps her fingers on the wooden edge. I shuffle to the table and try to lift a leg over the edge, but it's too heavy. The midwife grabs me under the arms and hoists me, pushing my lower half with her knee. From this vantage, I can see the whole room, like a bird in its treetop roost. Rusted coffee cans stacked by the stove, a chamber pot next to the mattress in the corner with a moth-eaten quilt thrown atop, a weathered copy of the Bible on a frayed quilt. I can hear my breath move through my teeth and lips, back in through my nose.

The midwife places a hand on my shoulder and guides me flat against the table. She pulls my dress over my knees, above my belly, slower and more gently than she did on her visit days before, as though she fears she might break something if she isn't careful. The soiled fabric bunches at the edge of my chin. She plants a palm on the ridge where my ribs begin and starts to count, her face pinched in concentration. I see her teeth, black and gray, tongue clicking against them. A loose one shifts with each click.

Still minutes apart, she says, finally releasing her hand. *I'm afraid you're in the early stages.* I've disappointed her again, from the look on her face. Pains too soon, then too slow.

Again she pushes down on my belly, counts.

I need to release the waters, to speed up the pains. They're too few and far between.

It feels like the pains are plenty, but I don't tell her that.

Wide, she commands, pointing to my legs. She rolls up a sleeve and points her index finger, jagged nail blackened with dirt, straight out in preparation. I wonder if she keeps her nail long like this, knowing what might be required of it. I wonder how many times she has used it for this purpose, all the other women she's punctured on their way to motherhood. I am but one face in a long line she's ushered through the threshold. Her hand disappears between my legs. She must succeed in breaking through, because a quick rush pours from inside and, as it flows, it strips the sinew and reduces me to bone. Time rushes at me, faster and faster, a swirling eddy. I may be losing myself in it, the way I am losing my limbs, which are growing ever more distant and numb.

When at last, during a fleeting break, I'm able to bend my neck up, I see that brownish greenish sludge has soaked my thighs, my legs, dribbled onto my feet. I must have lost my shoes somewhere along the way. In the outhouse? In the mud? At the doorstep to the house? Did the midwife remove them before I summited the table?

Why is it so dark? I ask, about the waters.

Devil's work, shade like that and all. Satan knows that a woman giving birth is a woman vulnerable. He strikes the weakest. Women are like the frontier, open and raw, and the devil must be a face the midwife sees lurking daily in the corners of her home, so it comes as no surprise seeing it leeching out of me. She yanks the newspaper from under my bottom, soaked through and disintegrating in her hands, crumples it and tosses it into the fire, which roars up at the new fuel.

It's growing dark. I hear the midwife sending someone away from the door, perhaps ordering her children to stay elsewhere for the night, or perhaps she's speaking to my husband, who's finally come to fetch me, or her husband home from his ministering, but her voice is so faint and distant it may be a dream and I can't hear the person to whom she speaks.

When the sun completely sets, she lights a gas lamp near the window, along with two tallow candles she places on either side of the table, framing me like an altarpiece. She does not bother to drape a blanket or fanout my skirts, which are still hitched up to my chest. Back home, great measures were taken to afford privacy. Sheets brought in specially for this purpose, draped over the knees. I remember my sister in a crisp pink gown and matching cap trimmed in lace, propped up against my mother's finest pillows. A beautiful display for such a wretched event. She has not been so beautiful since.

All my life until now had been an inhale, deep and long, a waiting for this very moment when I depart down a path towards mother or dead woman or mother to dead child. I'd seen it many times before, the forking of roads. How the woman enters the birthing chamber and is spit out on one side or the other. There's no telling which. You can't read a pain the way a fortune teller reads a palm or an orb. More like an alchemist with his metals—attempting to turn lead to gold—how sometimes the trick goes awry.

Dark whiskers twitch at the corners of the midwife's lips. The room waits, airless. An owl hoots. I think of the stars, studding the blackness. My sister's face grew so pale after the birth of her last, sickly daughter that her black eyes glowed against her skin, the inverse of a starry night. That daughter lived but six days. She flailed her scrawny limbs and hardly latched. Her lips cracked. The skin on her face slackened. My sister pressed her breasts together and caught the milk in a spoon to drop into the tiny, chapped mouth. The girl died alone in her cradle while her mother was busy, tending to the fire and the wash and the other children. She hadn't kept track of how long the baby had been sleeping, hadn't thought that in the quiet lull its breath was leaving its body altogether. She could not forgive herself.

I grab the midwife's hand because it seems an anchor and I fear I may float away. Bony fingers, skin covered in the filth of my body: brown sludge and red blood and other things I can't name, sticky and waxy and warm. *Something's gone wrong*, I say, through gritted teeth. Bile rises up through my throat and pours out of my mouth. I haven't eaten since before the pains began, before I fled to the outhouse; there's no food left inside to bring up. The sour liquid dribbles down my cheek and onto my neck. I don't have the strength for a proper vomit. I also don't have the strength to wipe it away with my sleeve, and the midwife doesn't bother with it, either.

An edge of black wing smacks the glass window at the top of the door, falls to the ground. *Stunned, not dead*, my husband likes to tell me about all manner of dead and dying creatures we see in the woods, though I know the truth is *dead not stunned*. In those moments I do not let on that he hides nothing from me. He presumes my innocence, that I'm frightened for the creatures and sad to witness their demise. Feminine emotion, that inborn fragility, getting the better of me. Truth is I understand this is the way of the world. I feel nothing in those moments but a sense of completion, a welling up of relief, even, to know that nature has run its course. A fox or cat will find the bird's body, an easy meal to be dragged off to a hollowed tree trunk or a den, dismantled, bones sucked dry of their meat.

As my belly grew wider and tauter and spring began to thaw the land, I walked the hills around the town, looking out for signs of violence, vultures hunting fresh corpses, beheaded rabbit carcasses hidden in the brush. I felt so animal, with this limbed and tender thing growing inside me. I could see it move under my skin: an elbow, a foot poking through. Sometimes I would stand and watch it for what seemed like hours, mesmerized, until it quieted down to sleep. I was no longer myself.

Something's wrong, I say again to the midwife, because there's a deep stabbing in my back, pushing through bone. I yearn to be the rabbit in the fox's mouth, quick pain over in one snapping motion.

Darling, something's always wrong. Is she mocking me? *This is what it means to be a woman. This*—she gestures towards me. The older women pride themselves on their experience. Present it as wisdom, tied in a neat bow, clucking at the young and their naivete. But now I can see that the midwife is as lost as I am. That she has no words to describe what is happening to me, what has happened or will happen to us all.

I bear down so hard when the next pain strikes that my jaw clamps and I hear a crack in the back of my mouth, a tooth split apart. The burning in my jaw melds with the cleaving in the rest of my body. I have become all pain. The midwife peers between my legs. She pushes down on the top of my belly, leans into her palm to apply more pressure. I see her bare feet, dirt-covered and calloused, walking up to my head, which she dabs with a wet rag.

Someone wails. I don't feel vibrations come out of my throat. The sound is too deep to be mine. If the wail were a chasm in the ground it would be wide; a person would die instantly if they fell in. The midwife stretches my legs apart. Nothing moves. Another tightening does not come. For a moment there is no pain at all.

I can see the head, she says. *The hair.*

Nothing budges.

Push harder with the next, she tells me.

Suddenly something grips me, moving through my feet my thighs my belly where the baby waits in the cavern of my womb, up into my chest, neck and head; the contents of my skull might burst out from the pressure. It's like canning, the way we seal the jars so tight no air stays behind and they let out a quick gasp when, months later, we finally unscrew the tops.

I push but not because I'm trying—my body has no choice but to bear down.

Push harder, child! Does she know I don't control my body any longer?

Push! Push!

There's silence.

Push!

She waits, then reaches a hand up and into me.

Something dislodges.

Silence.

She pulls.

Silence.

Something slips out of me.

Silence

Is it a baby?

Silence.

Could it be a baby?

Silence.

Is it mine?

The midwife grabs a pair of shears hanging on a hook by the hearth. She snips between my legs. Must be the cord. I don't see it happen but feel a tug.

The midwife holds what has come out against her bosom and turns away. *Don't look, child. Close your eyes.*

But of course I don't close my eyes. What kind of person closes her eyes to this? Certainly not a mother. Am I a mother?

The creature has exited me and vaulted over this world straight into another.

The midwife wipes at the body with the edge of her apron. *Do you want to know what it is?* I see the top of what must be a head, though so gray and misshapen it looks nothing like a head at all, more like a rotting cabbage.

The walls around me crumble faster and faster. Soon there will be nothing left around us. A sharpness lodges at the edge of my rib-cage. A pulsing begins at my head and waves through my body, over and over.

It was a boy, she whispers, though I haven't asked.

Chicago

Do you want to know what it is? **the doctor asks.**

What what is? I'm not sure what it looks like, the baby, but I can see it's the wrong color: bluish-brownish-green. No shade of living creature. The crowd of waiting pediatricians has descended on it.

It's a boy, the doctor says. *You have a baby boy.*

The doctor doesn't tell me she's revoking what she said about waiting a moment while they work on the baby and it feeling like eternity but that everything would be ok, it didn't mean that anything was wrong, and soon enough I'd get to hold the baby, and not to be alarmed. But when the pediatricians begin to leave the room with the baby, I understand this to be the case.

Congratulations! the doctor says, about the fact that it's a boy. Because this is the script we're supposed to be following. But I've forgotten my lines, and none of that matters anymore.

Peter Chamberlen, intent on keeping the details of his groundbreaking invention secret, would clear the birthing room, blindfold the patient. Only then would he extricate those gleaming forceps from their case and hold them up to the light. The woman would thrash, doubly disoriented by her pain and the sudden swallowing darkness.

Dr. G. has left and it's just me and Jed and the nurse with the plain face and plain name.

Was it a busy night? I ask the plain nurse, because I need to fill the thickening silence. The machines have stopped whirring. There are only our voices and the creak of footsteps.

About average, she says. *Yesterday, though, they were popping out one after another. Like they'd all gotten together and made a pact.* She smiles, grabs a tray of tools, pumps sanitizer into the cup of her hands, escapes into the hall.

Now that the baby is gone the action has moved outside of the room. Jed and I are stranded. We've been abandoned together, trying to make sense of where we've been deposited, which is both the same room we entered hours ago and a place completely unrecognizable. I watch Jed watch the door click shut behind the nurse, with a look on his face that tells me he's scared to be here, serving as my last tether to the outside world when he's also hanging on by a thread.

It's very important for both of us to feel empowered in this process, said the pregnant woman's husband to the doula at the coffee shop. He grabbed his wife's hand across the wrought-iron table, pushing a half-eaten muffin out of the way and claiming his place in her story, asserting his ownership. *For things not to just happen to us because the doctors say so.* The patio door slammed shut behind another café patron, clattering over the doula's response.

I refused to refer to the pregnancy as "ours." There was no "us" when it came to delivery. "We" were not pregnant, I would point out to Jed, and he'd laugh at how riled up this got me. This would be child as much as mine, of course, and I was determined to share the work of parenting, but I knew that pregnancy and delivery as a shared experience was a lie.

And I was right. As I pushed the baby out along with the tug of forceps, I was completely encapsulated in my own bubble, momentarily unaware of the throngs of doctors and nurses who'd gathered around, of Jed holding my hand next to me. I transformed into the blindfolded patient of Peter Chamberlen.

Some time after the arms and claws recede back into the walls, a new doctor walks in. His rubber-soled feet squeal across the floor. Dr. R. introduces himself with a formal handshake, as though at a gala. *I'm a neonatologist,* he says, hitching up his scrub. He sits down and scoots his chair to the bed's edge. Turns out he was one face in the wallpaper surrounding me when Baby was pulled out, when I was a specimen on display. He leans closer, believing proximity softens language, and explains data they gathered in the NICU (electrodes hooked to Baby's scalp, examination of reflexes and color and muscle; blood sifted and scored) while I tried to make my way back into my body, and the conclusion he'd drawn: lobes overtaken with snaking whiteness. Baby's brain: once whole, now hollow as a shell after the mollusk dies and slips from its salty berth. *Suspected brain injury,* he concludes, and I try to pull the blindfold tighter.

We stand in the middle of an empty field, nothing in the distance we can see, not even horizon. Around us weeds grow up and up and wrap around our limbs and circle our necks, tight and unforgiving.

The doctor explains that the baby needs to undergo a treatment for three days, after which time they will be able to determine the extent of the injury. For now, we have to wait. Dr. R. is slender and slightly hunched, with a sweep of blond hair and a small, pulsing Adam's apple. He's too diminutive to deliver this blow. He should be hulking, gruff, and deep. Because of this, I hate him with a vengeance that does not relent with time.

Dr. R. must leave. It's the end of shift. Other doctors will take over in the NICU, he says, but he wanted to break the news, for continuity's sake. I don't tell him he was a blur in the crowd and that there's no such thing as continuity. Still, he knows the baby he calls our son better than we do. He has held and touched him, seen his face and determined the course of his treatment. Jed and I are parents in name only. No, even that will not occur until hours later when the NICU receptionist attaches hospital bracelets to our wrists that read: PARENT/GUARDIAN. For now, we are figures fixed to the bed or field and other figures orbit.

Jed lowers the guardrail and scoots into the narrow bed with me. He presses his face to mine. Somehow, he knows I am splitting and is trying to hold me together. Now that the birth is over, the baby pushed out, he's resuming his place in the narrative. Now he can become a part of the process, like the father meeting the doula in the coffee shop desired. The baby Dr. R. diagnosed is Jed's, too, and so the pain of labor has transformed into the pain of whatever this new thing is; it's becoming ours to share. He squeezes me tight against his chest and I'm comforted by how desperate his grip is. I'm not the only one reeling and looking for something to steady myself against.

Just as there are two versions of me—in the bed and in the vent—there were two Peter Chamberlens—Elder and Younger. Historians debate which one was responsible for introducing forceps as a mechanism for live birth, for blindfolding the mother before saving her life along with her child's. Whether it was Younger or Elder, the invention was paramount, and the removal of the woman a necessary price to pay for its protection. The Chamberlen's were the premodern version of a baby brand, Uppababy or Dr. Brown's, patenting wares to protect profits. The veneers change, grow sleeker, focus-group tested—but at their core, it's all the same.

Has Dr. G. been lurking the whole time? Or has she just returned now that Dr. R. has left? The arms of her sweater flap as she opens a file.

When will they bring the baby back? I ask. Because perhaps the mild-mannered doctor's diagnosis was incorrect, and the baby's simply in shock. Doesn't that happen? Doesn't a newborn sometimes take time to figure out how to breathe? I feel like I've heard that before, somewhere, maybe one of those movies?

Didn't neonatology speak with you? she replies. I can't tell if she's mystified or annoyed by my question, or if she just wants to avoid having to talk about the baby.

I nod, and before I can say more she begins explaining something else: my own toxicity. The cure, delivery, has occurred, but now they must administer magnesium through an IV drip to stabilize my body and prevent the onset of seizures. *Mag,* she calls it, similar to her nickname for the baby's meconium, *mec*—diminutives used to denote serious things.

Nothing tells me I'm sick except her proclamation. Like the narrowing flow around the baby that drained his brain white, this brewing catastrophe is also silent, unfelt, registering only as faulty numbers on the hospital's set of lab results.

HELLP syndrome, Dr. G. explains, is one of the many aspects of maternal and postpartum health that remain poorly understood. The thinking, she says, is that this disease has its roots in the placenta, that transient organ fashioned for and then expelled with the baby who is not mine, and, I am quickly learning, the culprit behind much of what can go wrong in pregnancy. Once it leaves in the third stage of delivery, the afterbirth, the body can begin to heal. There's no other cure. Because of my condition and the baby's (though Dr. G. only wants to discuss my illness; she is no longer responsible for the baby), they'll be sending the placenta to pathology. Sealed in a medical waste bag, I imagine, then slivered and arranged on a slide and examined under a microscope.

But it's not my illness and not my baby. The hospital confuses. Strips clothes. Numbs bodies. Removes organs. Overlays foreign language on the once-familiar. Blindfolds. I thought this treatment of women as hollowed-out Russian nesting dolls rather than full people was a relic of the past, that birth had evolved, that society had progressed. I did not realize that birth is stepping into a time machine and traveling backwards.

Medical research today sidelines pregnant women, supposedly out of fear of hurting their fetuses. No institution wants to sign off on expecting women as research subjects, so pregnancy and its complications remain understudied and shrouded in questions. HELLP syndrome, along with its cousin, preeclampsia, is understood more like a vibe, a gestalt, than an exact mechanism defined by cause and effect. It's got something to do with circulation through the placenta gone awry, but it's hard to say exactly what is happening or why it occurs, and therefore it's basically impossible to treat with more than the equivalent of bandages. This kind of vague gesturing might be at home in art criticism but is less welcome in science. The exception is the field of women's health, which in spite of its name understands shockingly little about the female body.

Generations before me, women gave birth under twilight sleep. A potent cocktail of medications—morphine to dull the pain and scopolamine to scrub the memory—converted her into a doll, limp and malleable, memory-less. The drugs settled in and blitzed her into a body emptied of conscious thought. Labor could then course through without doctors having to bother with her pains and fears and desires. Birth without mother, as the baby's medical records contend.

This was all the rage. The rich in particular flocked to the procedure. They saw it as a way to maintain their ladylike status, uphold their façade as creatures too dainty and demure to withstand the visceral, animal attack of birth. The fact that they couldn't cope with the pain was proof positive of their cherished femininity and evolved status. They needed to be lifted above the impurities and indignities that had historically accompanied childbirth. For a time, twilight sleep was crowned the crème de la crème of delivery. The goal: to cloak the experience in the impenetrable, to make it as though it hadn't happened, except as a blurred dream just out of reach. No evidence but for the sleeping bundle of baby ushered in when the woman woke from her spell.

I'm sister to these blitzed women. The forceps must have scooped me out of my body along with the baby. I experience the inverse, a postpartum twilight; where they woke after birth, I go to sleep.

The baby's medical records describe a "vaginal delivery with forceps assist, after a pregnancy complicated by maternal HELLP (treated with magnesium), maternal ITP prior to pregnancy. Delivery was complicated by meconium staining of amniotic fluid, and meconium was suctioned from below vocal cords."

I am not a character except by indirect inference. I'm a shadow without a fully fleshed body. The term "mother" becomes the adjectival "maternal," which only modifies malignant conditions. Maternal is the harbinger of danger and also mysteriously absent from the birth, which is turned so abstract it's drained of action, declawed and denuded. The records make me a dissociated prerequisite from which complications, but not a baby, flow. Things happen, unstoppable, rolling, driven by invisible forces. Do hospitals know their attempt to cleanse the narrative excises subjects and replaces humans with their syntactic ghosts? The records are the written equivalent of twi-light sleep, pushing the mother out of the way. The scopolamine and morphine have been discarded but they cast a long shadow that even the doula's halcyon promises can't overtake.

Omissions of the mother date back to well before the advent of twi-light sleep. A set of 600-year-old illustrations of fetuses depicts their bodies (drawn as shrunken adults in that way of so much medieval art) nestled in the balloon of the uterus; in several they're folded into a V, arms outstretched, falling like Don Draper in the *Mad Men* opening credits. The drawings don't show mothers at all. They're reduced to outlines of their wombs. Only good for parts.

Dr. G. also has to leave. Her shift is over, just as Dr. R's is. Apparently it's the next day. We arrived one morning and now it's the following. The sun set and rose but I didn't observe the shift. I no longer care what day it is. I don't know if the lake still sits outside the win-dow. Same goes for the street and bus stop and office building across from the hospital with hundreds of other doctors and patients in and out of elevators and doors, and, across the river and highway, our apartment, pajamas still strewn on the bathroom floor and laundry clumped in the dryer and coffee congealing in a pot on the counter.

I'm sorry, she says, about the leaving. Her black clogs clank away. Jed and I are stuck here, alone yet again. Both of us are in the bed, holding each other. Unlike the doctors, I cannot exit the room or the hospital. I can't flee the new domain I've entered: not quite mother-hood but also not *not* motherhood. If he wanted to, Jed could stand up, say he has to stretch his legs, go get a Coke from the vending machine. Did the husband at the coffee shop know this? That he could stake his claim and then leave any time he wanted? But Jed is now part of this, and so he doesn't. He stays, curled beside me.

It's strange that a person can damage their brain before they're born, I say to the nurse with the plain face and plain name when she returns for a check. The statement is more philosophical than personal. That's how wrong it is, how beyond the rules of the universe, that a body can endure such injury before breathing air. It's an abstract assertion, hollowed out, posed as thesis. I imagine the injury as a strong suction, pulling the brain matter out through a long tube. The shape of the head remains, an empty vessel.

The nurse holds her expression—mouth a flat line, eyes staring ahead (not cruel, steady) and busies her hands with buttons and cords and papers. Her face the sort of plain that's impossible to decode. *Anything can get damaged*, she says, *anytime.* Jed doesn't say anything. There's nothing he can say that will comfort.

It's strange, too, that a body can experience the aftereffects of pain without feeling the cause of the pain itself. Now that the baby is out and the epidural removed, I'm beginning to sense where labor carved through me. The epidural's numbing was temporary. Similarly, the morphine given during twilight sleep didn't erase labor pains entirely. Nothing can. Women sometimes thrashed, in spite of or because of the drugs, and if the thrashing was violent enough, they had to be restrained in railed beds—cribs, really, for grown women. The second drug of the cocktail, scopolamine, scooped out her memory along with the baby. The woman might experience pain in her body, but she wouldn't remember it—or at least that was the hope. The doctors could take comfort from this, because did the pain count if it didn't linger? Without memory, was it real? Did it happen?

The transport team arrives. The plain-faced nurse waves goodbye as they move me from bed to wheelchair so they can push me out of the delivery room and off the delivery floor and into a postpartum room on the postpartum floor, making space for the next woman. I'd been rationed excess time here amongst the steel arms while the plain-faced nurse attempted to arrange a visit to the baby. But still the baby isn't ready for viewing, and again I've reached my limit. The women here are commodities, empty bodies, names and dates of birth for insurance reimbursements. The staff has to keep us moving in order to pay the bills. I want to shout at each person who flits past and remind them that we should have moved on from twilight sleep.

I want to tell them who I am, relay the facts of my life—that thing that seems to have ground to a halt with no warning.

We start down the hall. Jed follows. I look back and see him, hunched over in defeat, dragging our suitcase with one hand, unopened camera bag slung over the other shoulder. His steps are heavier than before, when he walked behind me from triage to labor and delivery. The suitcase rounds the bend and catches on a corner. He hardly seems to notice. We pass room after room of women laboring and birthing. I am no longer laboring or birthing, I have to remind myself. I've been emptied of all that. The hallway shrinks to a dark tunnel.

On the hospital tour with expectant parents, the instructor brought us to see the prime postpartum suite: a corner room with uninterrupted views of the lake. Between bed and window sat a glass bassinet where the baby could sleep soundly while the parents regarded their newborn and, in the process, glimpse the vast, sparkling lake in the background. Everyone asked, *How do we get this? Can we request it ahead of time?*

Before, in a classroom downstairs, we'd reviewed the stages of labor and delivery, protocol for arrival at the hospital, ways to distinguish false labor from real. When it was time for questions, a woman who detested the thought of an epidural because it impinged on natural processes asked our instructor how to avoid one. Another, terrified of pain, wanted to know how quickly hers could be administered. Both, though, desired this room. It was the hospital's version of the Uppababy stroller, the luxury item everyone covets. *There's no way to request it,* the instructor smiled. It was obvious she got this question a lot. *Luck of the draw.*

After the tour we returned downstairs to watch a video of a doctor scooping a screaming infant from its mother, placing it on her chest. All the women in the class cried (hormones, motherhood). The men grinned, as if regarding the preserved specimens of their wives from outside a glass case. They could observe emotion, not touch it. Like the husband interviewing the doula, they thought they should be a part of the process, but only wanted in up to a point. I couldn't see Jed's face—he was right next to me. I knew he'd be less smug than the others, but still, he probably remained on one side of the glass barrier. Now, though, I know he's crossed into the case.

The transport team delivers me to the containment room on the postpartum unit, which I think is several floors above labor and delivery but might be several below. Centuries ago, Chamberlen's blindfold did this same work of disorienting now left to efficient infrastructure (elevators and hallways and keycard-operated swinging doors). The magnesium begins to settle in. IV attached to arm, bag hanging above, emptying itself out, drip by drip, an hourglass. A neuroprotectant meant to shield my brain from my body's toxicity. Back in the cavernous delivery room, as the nurse hung the bag of fluid on the stand, she explained how it would make me feel as though I'd suddenly fallen ill with the worst flu of my life.

Or maybe a new nurse hangs it now, after we've ascended (or descended) to the new floor. Regardless, no one warns of hallucinations.

Close your eyes, rest, the nurses and doctors tell me, because they need to check off the assess-mental-wellness-and-offer-corresponding-advice box. I can feel tears on my face but I'm hardly aware that I am crying; the tears have quickly become a part of me, like skin or nails. Now, instead of mother, I'm a liability. I try to heed their advice, but when my lids flutter shut, I hear disembodied voices. I listen hard to decode their strange language.

I open my eyes and see nothing.

They're not real.

Eyes shut and the voices return. They're real.

I open my eyes and the voices turn off.

Shut again; they return.

Eyes open and they stop.

But I can't keep my eyes open forever. I haven't slept in nearly two days and the lids keep closing against my will, letting the voices stream back.

The world is halved: one part bathed in harsh-bright light, objects sharply defined but stilled by thick silence; one part unintelligible grumbling and babbling and moaning beneath surface of darkness. I exist on two parallel planes.

Did the women of twilight sleep ever notice their two planes—of twilight stupor and conscious awareness—collide? Did they feel slivers of dormant, unhinged memory suddenly pierce random moments of their days? The shiver of shears against their necks at the salon or the shrill beeps of morning alarm clocks? How did they make sense of these shards: plotless, out of time, artifacts of an unknown event? Peter Chamberlen's patients, too, perhaps, felt the cold slap of metal on an arm or leg and they knew it was familiar, knew it evoked another time and place; but, having been blindfolded from the minute the forceps were pulled from their case, they could not place the sensation, only knew that it triggered panic, a fear that they were about to lose themselves. The worst sort of déjà vu.

Do I hear someone say, *The first day of your child's life feels like the last of your own?* I am waking. Magnesium tingles in my bones. I have no baby. Have not met him and have not held him, could not pick him out of a nursery line-up. I should leave the hospital with my still-packed suitcase. The baby belongs to doctors, to machines, to this sterile place, and so they should keep and care for him. My baby is an empty space, a waiting. I have not asked for a broken child, have not prepared myself for this iteration of motherhood. I am also an empty space. I see myself, years from now, pushing a wheelchair down a dark and silent hallway. Where is the boy? Maybe they will never hand him over. I don't tell anyone any of this because a mother is supposed to love at all costs.

In the yoga studio where we pretended—or maybe believed—our bodies would soon be treated as whole, solid things, we closed our eyes and lowered our heads. The yoga instructor chided: *greet your thoughts without judgment.* She had no idea.

The body in the bed remains halved, top fully felt, bottom tingling as sensation begins to return. The voices continue. Each time I close my eyes they start out sounding vaguely familiar. If only I listen closely, I might be able to understand what they're saying. But as soon as I try, they crumble into chaos. The more I listen, the more incoherent the voices grow, the more I try to decipher them. I end up feeling like a broken machine, unable to decode, stuck in the loop.

Adrienne Rich writes: *a woman's fantasies of her own death in childbirth have the accuracy of metaphor.* She speaks of how the modern woman swaps the very real historical fear of death from puerperal fever and other preindustrial complications for abstract fear of identity eclipsed by a child. But this flattening I feel is not abstract. Premodernity is barreling over me. The flattening has removed me from my own body and my own timeline, thrown me back. I emerged from the delivery room into the historical world Rich treats as distant inheritance, vague epigenetic memory. Around me its edges solidify into three-dimensional shapes.

Wild West

The midwife rubs the back of the cabbage-headed baby. The weak flick of her wrist tells me she doesn't believe it will make a difference. It's a performance for my sake, or hers. The baby's waxy neck shines. Its substance has evaporated. The body is empty. The midwife stops her rubbing. She blows into the baby's face. It doesn't flinch. She lifts an arm. It flops down.

I let out a small noise. I want to reach out and touch the baby. I want to nuzzle its head against the edge of my chin. I want to hold its deflated hand up to the dim candlelight and examine its nailbeds and the thin bridge of skin connecting the thumb to the rest of the fingers. I want to rest its head on my chest and let it sleep there. My chest? I have almost forgotten about this part, about the milk. My chest aches, but it's more of a searing underneath my ribcage, not the swelling of milk I've been told of. Could milk coax something like life back into this floppy body? Could a dead baby's lips coax milk into the breasts? I imagine them filling up with the creamy liquid, round and tender, small trickles of gold dribbling out. *Baby, come eat!*

I understand if I were to speak these thoughts aloud they would be nonsense, the ramblings of a madwoman. Having crossed over into the realm of mother to dead baby, sense no longer has a place. A madwoman is a woman living in the between, with the knowledge that there's more than this material world. Grief is another word for mad is another word for wisdom or at least wisdom-seeking. A madwoman simply wants to know. *Baby, are you there? Can you eat? Can I feed you? Are you there? Are you there? Are you there?*

I lost one, too, the midwife says, her voice nearly kind. She turns her back to me and walks to the bureau on one side of the room. She bends over and her arms move back and forth, wiping, folding. She turns around to face me, her handiwork displayed on top of the bureau. What was once the baby is now wrapped tightly in a brown cloth, tattered but clean. The bundle of baby could be a hunk of pork or dough set out to rise. None of the body remains exposed. It seems cruel, the way she's covered its nose and mouth. Does it feel suffocation? I try to sit up to get a better look, to see if some small corner of flesh pokes out, but my body does not obey. I feel the pulse of energy sent from my brain to my back and sides and arms but nothing happens. My head tightens, a band across my forehead like it's also wrapped in cloth. I put a hand up to feel it but of course there's nothing there. Just slick sweat, matted hair.

Anyway, no use mourning. This world is too harsh for these small souls. With Jesus now. The voice drones, like the chugging rumble of trains in the distance as they approach the depot. *With Jesus now,* she says again. *We'll see them soon enough, when we get to His kingdom.*

I can tell she doesn't believe what she says. Heaven repels unrepentant, unbaptized souls—she of all people must know this. Probably she thinks the babes are cast into the fiery flames of damnation.

What would the midwife say if she knew I was a Jew by birthright, and so the baby is too? Does that make the baby's fate worse? My mother told me her mother was a Jew on her deathbed, whispering so my father in the next room wouldn't hear. It didn't matter that we went to church, she said, because it was a thing passed down through mothers the way one inherits an amulet. I had no choice in the matter. I was saddled with it, ox-like. Her mother had told her and her mother's mother had told her and now she was telling me. Later, we buried her in the churchyard with a cross carved into her headstone. I wore black and knelt beside her grave in prayer and kept my promise to hold close this secret. My father's family would have never let them marry, my mother told me, they would cut us all off if they found out, she said. She'd pretended to be an orphan when she met him and before she knew it, she was in too deep. It wasn't difficult, she said, to play the part. At least not for a while.

The invisible vise on my head tightens. *You look pale.* The mid-wife places the back of her hand on my brow but I can't feel it.

I hover off the table. As I rise, the vise loosens, my head discon-necting from the rest of me.

A happy shriek sounds from the woods. Farther away: hoots, hoofs. *Independence Day,* the midwife explains, unprompted. *Must be midnight.* Each year the town turns festive on the fourth: hogs roasted on spits, musicians plucking out-of-tune fiddles, guns shot skyward. On the frontier the men seize this opportunity to celebrate their freedom, manifest in the wide-open spaces, theirs for the tak-ing—no matter that there were others here, tending this land, long before. They see it as theirs for rambling through on horseback, for studding with rails and wagon trails, for hunting down the wild crea-tures of the hills. Here there is room to grow families, their women fruitful and multiplying like God intended. God gave them this vast and desolate land, which will, in time, with enough sweat and blood, become the new promised land, and soon their sacred flags will fly high above it all.

The women–the respectable ones, at least–never join these cele-brations. The women, even the young girls not yet married off, know the frontier is not a vast realm of possibility but a limbo, a suspension between one state and the next. They watch from porches and bal-conies, lean their heads out of windows, as their sons and husbands hoot and holler and gallop through the town center, circle the tavern and blacksmith shop and jail and tall gallows that sit empty and wait-ing like an old man's gummy mouth, except when they aren't, when crowds gather round to watch the weathered convicts—highway robbers and stickup men—writhe from their nooses, feet scrabbling air. Another sort of town celebration, watching breath leave a body.

The midwife appears again, as if from nothing. The world keeps flashing black, then lighting up again. *I'm going to check you, down below.* She squats between my still-open legs and stays for what seems like hours, poking, prodding. I am losing track of time, seconds and minutes escaping. From the corner, the bundle of my dead baby beckons. *There,* she says, as something globs out of me. A splatter against the tin pan that she balances on her knee. *The afterbirth has come away, finally. Sticky thing it was.*

She sets the tin pan on the sill. The sun is beginning to rise. It glows against the viscous organ, a piece of me sitting outside of my body. It's strange to see myself there, to regard my insides the way I would look at a rock or a flower. It's not beautiful. It's meat, veined and dark. *That's what we are, meat, veined and dark*, the madwoman inside me says.

My body grows limper. The midwife takes a rag and wipes my face with cold water. She rubs my ankles to relieve the swelling. She paces the room, back and forth, blocking my view of the dead baby bundle. With her steps the floor creaks and the afterbirth quivers. *There you are*, the madwoman says, about the afterbirth.

Bad blood, the midwife mutters. Not to me, but to the basket in which she fumbles. *Nothing else to do.* She pulls out a knife. She wipes the rusted edge against her apron. The baby's wrapped body calls out to me, low and deep. A vibration not a voice. I would reach for it if I could. Hold it and let it suckle at my bosom.

Can you nurse a dead baby? the madwoman inside me asks.

Can you nurse a dead baby? I ask the midwife. I can feel the milk filling out my breasts.

What was that you said?

Can I feed him?

Have you gone mad? she asks, not unkindly.

I hear something rattle, metallic, in my skull. A rage taking root. My sight shaking loose. The stove blurs. Colors flash. The afterbirth shrouds in shadow. The floor breaks into pieces–the walls, too. I am crumbling farther and farther away from this body and its senses. What is left is a fiery wrath, distilled to its purest form, that wants to reach across for the baby that should be mine.

The midwife grasps my arm with one hand and with the other pushes the dull blade through the skin near the elbow. She squeezes her fingers into a cuff at the top of my arm to push the blood down and out through the opening. It dribbles into the chamber pot she's placed below. I feel nothing.

The midwife's breath is burnt coffee and canned fish and tooth rot. With a rush, I remember the smell of slightly burnt bread in my mother's kitchen back home and the talcum my father used after his shaves. I want to ask what the baby smells like. But I can no longer speak.

The blood continues to come, though not as fast as she wants it. She makes another cut into my flesh, this one deeper than the first, though still I feel nothing. I start to shake, but I am leaving my body. Part of me floats above. I watch the body below fluttering like a moth. I am the body and I am not the body at the same time.

One moment the midwife stands in front of me, so close I can still see the fat of her arm jiggling beneath her blue-veined skin as she prods at me, though the rest of the room is blurred. The next she's gone. The blur has taken over completely. In her place is not blackness but nothing. This must be blindness, which is different from how I'd imagined it. It's not scary or dark. I am not lost in it. It simply is.

You're gone, I say, maybe to the midwife, maybe to the dead baby, maybe to the body that was once mine. Maybe to no one.

I've seen this before, she announces, into the nothing. *You're hardly the first. Comes on fast, a mercy in its way,* she says.

There is only longing: to hold the baby, to feed it, to smell it. Angry yearning so deep it wants to rip me apart, is ripping me apart, though I have no corporeal form to rip. Regardless, the yearning is stronger than the pains of labor.

Do you want me to say a prayer for you? she asks, knowing full well I can't answer. She's a preacher's wife. She has to ask. She starts to murmur. I can't make out the words.

Where are you now? I ask the baby.

I listen. Silence.

I'll find you, I tell him. *Once I leave this place, I'll find you. Wherever you are.* It sounds like a threat, though I mean it as a comfort.

I'll find you. I'll find you. I'll find you.

Chicago

My new bed on the postpartum floor is in a containment room reserved for people with dangerous, communicable diseases. It features steel double doors and a blinding white hallway separating me from the chatter of other patients and the squeals of their healthy red things. It's no accident that they've put me here. My body's toxicity isn't contagious but my mind's might be. I imagine the women who preceded me as tenants, the various tragedies that made them not quite mother enough for a regular room. This is the purgatory of the recovery floor.

Doctors enter hourly, knead my abdomen so the uterus will deflate back into its clenched position. *This will hurt,* they say, and it does. A catheter discharges urine into a transparent bag hanging off the side of the bed. *I can tell you're well-hydrated,* a matronly postpartum nurse jokes; I don't laugh. She steadies me in the bathroom and swaps soaked pads for fresh ones, helps me pull up the mesh underwear holding it all in place. Jed waits outside the semi-closed door though he's seen all that came before; maybe he can tell the nurse doesn't want him in there, that she's territorial and wants to do her work efficiently, without pestering spouses, or maybe he's afraid of seeing me broken. She pours painkillers the shape and color of candy from small plastic cups into my palm then marks the swallows off on her sheet. Always she scans the barcodes so the doses can be added to the bill. She exudes perfunctory competence and doesn't acknowledge the absence of a baby in the room.

I didn't anticipate the sense of sudden aging I feel—elevator, cables cut, freefall. There's pain, though the medications take the edge off, and my legs and feet remain partly numb as the epidural takes its time to wear off. I'm only tangentially aware of my physicality. The magnesium, its fever-like vise on me, the way I come and go from the dark place of strange voices, paints everything I see and hear in a delirious wash.

Jed calls his parents. He manages: *You have a grandson.* He paces in front of the containment room door. From the other end of the phone rushes the excited, muffled jumble of their voices. *No. Stop, stop. Please stop. Let me talk,* Jed says. His voice crumbles. I can see he's bracing himself to get through the call, tightening every muscle. He's six-foot-two but suddenly looks so small and fragile, paper-like and foldable. When he hangs up, he collapses next to me, his entire frame heaving. I hold him against the body, plied with magnesium and painkillers and epidural remnants, a body that no longer belongs to me.

While we hunched in cat/cows, the yoga instructor said: *Your body tells the story of your life.* But what if it doesn't? What if you get pushed out of your body and you don't know what holds the story of your life anymore? The body is too fallible a container to hold so much.

After *Godspell* I asked the rabbi who taught our Sunday school class what Jews believe happens after death. Death had lately become a preoccupation of mine, sparked in part by the visceral death of Jesus I saw performed on stage over and over again. *Oh God, I'm dying,* he sang.

　We don't believe in heaven, per se, the rabbi told me. *Not in the Christian sense, at least. In the Jewish version of afterlife, people live on through memories.*

　Memory is memory and life is life and he meant to take the edge off the discomfort of existing in the physical world—cloaked in a heaving, sweating, pulsing body—one moment, disappearing forever the next. I didn't believe him. No one lives through memory. I could've explained this to the rabbi, but I was polite and a good student and didn't want to go against these two conceptions of myself, even in declaration of truth. Did this make me a coward?

I wonder what the rabbi would have said about this state I now inhabit. Would he have deemed it life or memory or something else? To me it feels like a mashup. I'm experiencing life as though it were already memory—the moments lack the crispness of present events, and the self is a removed spectator and not an actor.

I cannot describe the aging of the mind, also called grief, except that I picture the Edward Munch painting hovering over my hospital bed, the subject's hands clasping hollowed cheeks, vortex of red and blue encroaching from behind. While he tries to scream, sound vaporizes into color.

I spent many years after that conversation with the rabbi secretly wishing to be Christian. I craved comfort from an intervening god. I craved a workaround for death. The Jewish god I knew sat and watched people suffer. Not vengeful and wrathful in the way of stereotypical Old Testament portrayals—bearded man in the clouds shouting down in a booming bass—just distant and unconcerned. You could pray to him, ask for things, but no one believed it made any difference.

Many Jewish texts, when they do engage with the concept of afterlife beyond the tepidness of living on through memory, use the term "world to come." Perhaps "afterlife" is bound by the notion of a resurrected, physical Jesus on his throne and the material strictures of this world. Afterlife I see as a version of this world slightly elevated from the surface of earth, gussied up with fluffy clouds and intense rays of light; the world to come occurs in an altogether different dimension. The world to come I can't picture because it rejects the imposition of this life's concepts—houses or cousins or gardens or love—even as metaphor. It shuns human imagination.

This is not dissimilar from the Jewish notion of the divine. Unlike Jesus, who takes up residence in a human body and forges a direct connection to his followers, the contemporary Jewish god can only be approached indirectly, like an eclipse. Today's Judaism has no analog to the Christian concept of a personal relationship to Christ, this idea that people should cultivate individualized prayer practices or see the hand of Jesus in day-to-day occurrence.

I don't pray in the containment room, though I do consider my ancestors, how I feel more connected to their world than the tidy world of fit mothers in the yoga studio, or the ones I imagine down the hall watching their rosy, snuggled bassinets, rooting in their sleep. Surely life in the shtetl was full of despair. Not only the pogroms, the humiliation and persecution I learned about up from rewatching *Fiddler on the Roof* on a loop as a kid, but the more ordinary stuff too—illness, deprivation, the literal roof caving in during a storm. In thinking back towards these faceless figures as a comfort, a way of materializing company in this lonely and sterile place, I unwittingly attempt my own version of prayer.

The no-nonsense postpartum nurse wheels a contraption to my bed. *This will help your milk come in*, she says, which is her way of acknowledging our situation. The magnesium still courses through me, alongside the painkillers, and her voice wobbles. About milk I've forgotten entirely. The pump insists on my physicality. Can I reinhabit this body for long enough to use it? The nurse opens a plastic bag of sterile parts and begins her assembly. It seems impossibly complicated. She manipulates my breasts into the flanges. I watch like a distant onlooker. The machine switches on with a whirring sound—something from an industrial farm, animals crowded into putrid pens. I look for milk droplets but all I see is the brownish-reddish molt of nipples flaking under suction. *Rusty pipe,* narrates the nurse, tapping her nails on the side of the bottle, as though I've morphed from person to decaying infrastructure.

A museum in Vienna houses preserved fetuses who died at or before delivery. Lena Herzog photographed the specimens for *The Paris Review*. She wrote, "The Russian Orthodox church declared the souls of these babies 'lost'—they had no place in hell, heaven, or limbo. They were dead on arrival and had nowhere to go." Her ethereal pictures document: one hand like an empty glove except with nails;

a face with an open mouth searching; two faces pressed against each other, nestled in conversation. There is something off about the photos, alien and even monstrous (a word that appears in the thesaurus entry for "abnormal fetus"), but also they're deeply and undeniably human. The babies meander against a black backdrop, suspended. In the containment room while I wait to see my baby, I picture him like this: inhabiting an existence between born and not, frozen in time and space, while I inhabit a space between grief and motherhood, life and memory.

Jewish trepidation around pregnancy extends beyond contemporary superstitions like eschewing the baby showers or delaying crib construction and into Jewish rules and ritual. It used to be that birth was a crapshoot. You might get a live baby; you might not. Judaism evolved around this fact. Later, the nostalgia of the natural birth movement conveniently forgot it.

Jewish law, for instance, permits abortion up until the quickening, after that if the mother's life is at risk. A fetus simply isn't a person. A miscarried or stillborn baby, or an infant who dies during the first month of life, does not merit the same kind of mourning required for an older child or adult. The family doesn't sit shiva or pray the mourner's kaddish for this loss, which is not deemed a complete loss. The baby's body must be buried directly in the ground. The rabbis presumably thought their rules a kindness, mercifully preventing families from spending their entire lives mourning. Judaism has no concept of purgatory or limbo, and the specifics of the world to come are shaky, as indicated by my childhood rabbi, but it does have this: gradations of what it means to be a human, to be alive, as a protective salve against the world's terrors.

Labeled buttons on the phone beside my bed offer links to the world outside the double doors. Cafeteria: 1, Gift shop: 2, Chaplain: 3. A choose-your-own-adventure. I don't want to eat and I close my eyes hard at the glimmer of balloons and sprawling floral arrangements passing in the distant hallway on their way to celebrate mothers of healthy babies. But the orange blinking light beside the receiver demands attention, and the chaplain seems the only option.

The chaplain's name is Paul—a rabbi with the name of a Christian saint. He twitches and shifts uncomfortably the minute he steps inside the containment room. "I'm sorry," he says. Everything about him is slightly rumpled—his beard and his clothes—and I feel like something must be wrong with me for noticing these petty details on this particular day. He angles himself toward the door as he speaks, plotting his escape from this void. He's used to death, probably, but not this, whatever this is.

Hospitals have neatly partitioned spiritual care from medical. But medieval training of midwives involved equal parts administration of baptismal rites and medical instruction. If a mother died during delivery, her baby had to be quickly extracted to facilitate the soul-saving ceremony in the nick of time. Spiritual and medical on equal planes. Or spiritual edging out medical, with the medical subjugated as a route to a spiritual destination. Except I suppose midwives did not perceive this divide. They saw no distinction between realms. The separation was imposed later, by modernity. Back then, when the two worlds of here and after slammed up against each other with such force, it was nonsense to try to pry them apart. Babies shuttled from unborn to born, sometimes touching death in the middle before returning, sometimes settling there. Mothers, too. The midwives worked in the space of world-mixing. They ferried souls back and forth between the porous boundaries.

The hospital, though, has strict boundaries: delivery and postpartum; newborn nursery and neonatal intensive care; medical and pastoral. The nurses are careful to avoid contamination with careful cleaning protocol. I'm kept behind double doors. They don't want anything to cross from one side to another. I yearn for a place with more leniency, where someone can shepherd me through this in-between: I am a mother and not a mother; my baby is alive and not alive; this is happening to me now and also it's already a memory. There are no midwives at the ready to save my soul.

We wait in containment-room limbo to meet the baby. He's still the baby of the hospital. *He's not stable yet*, the matronly nurse tells us, without elaborating. I don't know what questions to ask to help me better understand what it means for a newborn to be unstable. So I don't ask. I wait. I pump every two hours, as instructed. I get nothing, more nothing, and more nothing. *It takes time,* the nurse says, when she comes over and examines the bottles. *Don't give up.* I can't give up. There's nowhere to go and nothing to do. I'm stuck in this room pumping emptiness out of my body for a faraway baby.

I am lying in the bed in the double-doored room on the postpartum floor without the baby and I am in the vent of the delivery room as the baby is being born and then as the baby is out but I can only see that it is misshapen and the wrong color and then it is taken away and I am standing in an empty field with weeds gnarling around my body while the doctor with a sweep of blond hair explains my baby's impossible fate. I am in all of these places and I am nowhere. I feel the pain of my body but from a distance. I am not sure it is still my body and yet there's the pain creeping back in as the anesthetic leaves, so it must be my body. Perhaps this is a version of the afterlife, an impossible jumble of realities, collision of all possible realities, keeping one from inhabiting any reality at all. An existence entirely set in the interstitial.

Wild West

Brightness swarms the room. This was supposed to be the day I met my child, but I have yet to regard his face. Where is he? My body lies on the table, skin marbling with an exquisite purplish red. Now that I am no longer tethered to my body, the pain has evaporated, the breaking has ceased and some form of consciousness is restored. I float above the room and can see everything at once: the doctor hovering over my body, his shirt taut over his potbelly, pulling back my eyelids and peering into the pupils, lowering his ear down to my mouth to see if he can feel breath and pulling a sheet over my face when he can't; the midwife wiping down her rusty tools and gathering her soaked rags in a tin bucket for the washing; my husband standing at the doorway, taller than the rest and at attention like a stoic soldier; a rat scurrying at the edge of the scene, tempted by the thick stench of organic matter. From up here the world below appears shrunken.

A ring forms around where I float, a crowd of women's faces, other dead mothers, felled before and during and after birth. Dead from childbed fever and puerperal hemorrhage and septicemia. Dead from babies whose shoulders lodged in their too-small birth canals and had to be dismembered with crochet hooks, breaking something within the mother, too; and from thick and tangled afterbirths that refused to budge from the womb's wall. One dead from hanging herself in the weeks following delivery, a sudden descent of despair so great and deep and inexplicable; and another whose pessary—which the doctor placed below her deflated womb to keep it lodged inside her body—grew infected, the decay spreading throughout her body.

I know all this about these women with a simple glance. Together they let out a long moan, not of despair, but low and tender, warbling. A floating choir of pallid, long faces welcoming me, beckoning me, then fading away. Or else I fade into them, completing my transformation.

I scan the room and search for the bundle of my baby, but someone must have moved him already, in the gap during which I left the table and joined the mass of dead mothers. Don't they know I want to smell him? Where have they put him?

The midwife pulls a curtain across the window to keep the light out, maybe to give the room a proper sense of decorum, of mourning. Outside, the gunshots of the frontiersmen celebrating ring out. Even if they knew of our fates, a little tragedy would hardly stop this revelry. After all, each day there is something to mourn: an accident with an ax in the woods, cholera sweeping through a stretch of homes, a fall from a great height. I hear the gallop of horse hooves like a heartbeat, thrumming and urgent, accelerating. Was this the pace of my child's heart before it stopped, trying to save itself before time ran out? Is that why my pains grew so frantic at the end, piling up on each other until they spilled over?

The doctor and preacher and my husband, whose long, beard-patched face betrays no emotion, move my mottled body onto a cart. My husband holds my head in his hands, wide and calloused the way I remember them from life. He looks down at the head as though he wishes to say goodbye. There is a sadness in him, hidden away from the others, only meant for me. The doctor places the brown bundle with the baby's body at my feet. I long to touch it with a toe but I can no longer move this body, am no longer in the body at whose feet they place the baby's body.

The three men take turns pushing the cart along the path toward the doctor's home, the feet and head that once belonged to me spilling out over the sides as the wheels lurch over rocks and roots. With each jolt I hope the baby will move closer to my body, but the movement is not enough to make them touch. The load is heavy and when one man tires, another takes over. I follow, weaving in and out of the branches overhead.

In the woodshed, they heave the body up and place it in a pile of straw. It would scratch at my thighs and calves and elbows if I could feel. The idea of the itch claws at me, the little rough pieces poking the skin. I want to relieve it but cannot; besides, it is only the idea of an itch and not the thing itself, and an idea can't be scratched away. One side of the dress hikes up higher than the other, exposing a bloodied knee.

I try to imagine my husband upon first hearing the news of our demise, for which he had likely been preparing since my belly grew swollen with child. His own mother died in the days following her confinement with him, leaving him an orphan his whole life, to be raised by a succession of strict aunts and distant, impoverished cousins. Had the preacher been the one to break the news, knocking on the door of our cabin to narrate the course of events as his own wife had relayed them to him? He was bound to have gotten some details wrong in the transmission, perhaps the order of events or my last words. Along the way someone may have made up a final wish of mine so my death could become imbued with closure. No one likes a person dead without meaning. My husband would have listened from the threshold of our cabin, one foot in and one foot out, nodding solemnly, asking no questions. The edge of his mustache twitching ever so slightly the only sign of his distress.

The preacher doffs his hat and leaves the shed, begins to walk in the direction of his house. *I'll take the child for a postmortem*, the doctor says, greedily. My husband looks back at my body one last time, perhaps to get my approval, and wipes his hands on his oil-stained dungarees. He does not know I am floating above, not held within the body's skin.

If I've got your blessing, that is, the doctor adds, to urge my husband on. My husband nods. The doctor picks up the baby and drops the wrapped bundle in his satchel.

The two men exit. The doctor's satchel bobs with the weight of the baby. My husband pulls the door shut behind him. The latch clicks. My body remains alone in darkness. *That's it*, I think. And then I remember it's not over, though I may want it to be. I am tired.

But I have made a promise to my baby. It's the only thing we have left to tie us together, to make us more than two empty bodies. It's the only thing I have left to make me a mother. I try to open my eyes to look around, but the eyes of the body are no longer my eyes, and anyway, I can see without them. It takes time to grow accustomed to being outside of a body. I begin to adjust to the darkness.

Chicago

The baby's nurse calls my nurse to say the baby's finally ready for visitors. Some modicum of stability has been achieved. I don't want to go see him, not really, but I can't say this. There are some things a mother is not allowed to utter. I'm supposed to have been yearning for him from the moment of birth. Instead of yearning, I feel dread. I know that the longer I stay contained in my room, the longer this baby remains a baby of the hospital. I'm not ready to claim it as mine.

The epidural's effects are fading but my legs still droop. They're not ready, either. It can take time for them to reconstitute completely, I gather, imagining the nerve endings frayed and disorganized, searching for one another in the murky jelly of my body. Maybe the same thing is happening inside the baby. Jed and the nurse shift me out of the bed like a life-sized doll, arrange me upright in the chair, wheel me to the intensive care floor (protocol; I am a liability). I know Jed would understand my hesitation if I voiced it, the dread that surrounds me, which is connected to but different from the fear and grief I know he also feels, but I can't muster the energy to explain it. It's different from my cowardice when I talked to the rabbi years ago; I'm just too tired.

The chair clods over the elevator's lips. I grip the armrests; I might fall through the seat with each lurch. I'm no longer a solid thing. The trip from the postpartum floor to the NICU feels unending, though it's only a few corridors and one elevator ride away. No matter how much we move through the hospital, I have no sense of its topography.

We arrive at the NICU threshold. A receptionist emerges from behind a desk, finishes a call, places the phone down, jots a note, doles out white bracelets branding us parents. The plastic scrapes my skin as she fastens it in place and tightens the end. I don't mind. I welcome feeling things in my body that can momentarily draw me into the physical present. I expect her to look sad for us, for our situation, but her face holds itself still, inscrutable. This is her job, telling parents they are parents when they aren't, not really, then checking them for this marker of authenticity each time they enter. She presses a button and the locked doors to the unit swing open. She nods us through.

The nurse guides us past the clusters of regular NICU beds that stretch out behind a series of doors. We stop at the long hall's dead end, a private node labeled 1089B Mother/Baby Suite, which even I, muddled and half-numb, understand as code for *room for infants so critically ill they may not survive.* It's a euphemism for the nadir of the intensive care unit. 1089B is one of only a few suites lining the back wall of the NICU. The others are empty. There are no other babies as critically sick as ours, which must be a mistake, I think, in spite of all the evidence to the contrary—this whole thing a giant misunderstanding that keeps ballooning.

We walk through the sliding doors. Inside the suite, the baby they say is mine lies in an open glass box and wears a blue cap like a bicycle helmet, complete with a chinstrap to hold it in place. Ready for adventure, stuck in his glass box. He's a museum artifact on display. Eyes sealed shut, mouth clamped around a breathing tube. Everything about him is closed. Through the cap runs liquid, chilled to keep his body temperature down. *Therapeutic hypothermia*, his nurse calls it, gesturing for us to come closer. She says the words fast so we might not notice the oxymoron. No one can undo the brutal parching already inflicted, so now they try to freeze the torrent that follows. A fish gutted and splayed on ice pellets to stave off flies. Upstairs the mild-mannered doctor tried to explain that the injury itself was not over, or that there was one injury and then that injury could cause more injuries, but it didn't make sense, that an injury could be stopped and also keep going.

I stare down into the box. If I hadn't been led here, if I couldn't see the hospital ID on his ankle with my name on it, I wouldn't recognize this baby. I would be the mother in the hospital years ago, convinced her baby had been switched. The NICU team has cleaned him up—he's no longer the color of muck I saw from a distance in the delivery room, and his misshapen head hides underneath the cap. Jed seems to recognize him immediately, though. His body relaxes, shoulders lowering and breath slowing, for the first time since the baby emerged. There must be more paternal instinct at play than maternal. He reaches towards the baby but the NICU nurse motions for him to stop; the baby's not ready.

Baby will stay in this cap for three days, the nurse explains, *before we rewarm him.* Until this moment I believed the NICU held only incubators, tiny babies nestled inside. I didn't think of temperatures going in the other direction in a hospital, except in the basement morgue, freezers preserving flesh, did not know babies could require anything besides heat. This cold is not a recreation of the womb but a reversal of its embrace.

The baby's tiny fist knocks back and forth, rapping at an invisible door. His nurse presses a red button, like a Jeopardy buzzer. *He's having a seizure,* she explains, and despite the gravity of what she's explaining, she exudes warmth. She's trying to welcome us into this new, strange world as gently as she can. This too is parenthood, she means.

Are you sure those are seizures? I ask, because this is the only thing about the baby that makes him look alive.

Look, she says, and points. *The way you can tell it's a seizure is that the movement is rhythmic. Doesn't stop when I hold his arm down.* She places a hand on top of his to demonstrate. When she lifts, he continues knocking.

Will they stop? I ask.

We hope to get them controlled with medication, she replies. *But sometimes they return after cooling, when we rewarm the babies. It's hard to say.*

For the twelve hours of her shift, she sits on a stool and watches this hand for motion and, when it begins its telltale knock, she presses a button to release more sedative into his veins. If she needs a break, a surrogate must assume her place on the stool until she returns. *How boring,* I think, before stopping myself, reminding myself that this is my baby she is guarding, and that nothing here is mundane. I crave mundanity.

All the seizures, all suspicious events, get recorded for the chart—a folder already so thick that the next morning the new pediatric intern, hardly out of medical school and mere days into her residency in this winding, buzzing hospital, anxious to present on Baby Boy S. (not his last name; no one asked) in front of her attending, will drop it and watch the pages of data that tell the baby's story scatter across the floor. I will feel bad for her, embarrassed on her behalf, until I realize that my baby is a hurdle she must clear to prove herself, an obstruction standing between her and a good day at her new job, and my sympathy will freeze.

The gentle nurse cautions us against staying on the pullout couch in the Mother/Baby Suite, though that's ostensibly what it's designed for. *You won't get any rest,* she says. *There's no quiet here. You need rest to heal.* A good mother, I think, would insist on staying with her baby. But I listen to the nurse; I'm not sure I'm a good mother. I'm not sure I'm a mother at all, because I'm not sure this is my baby. Jed wheels me out.

William Smellie, a so-called "male midwife" in 1700s England, was rumored to conceal himself in women's apparel so he could sneak into deliveries where he was unwelcome. This was in the era before men were commonplace in birthing chambers, before they shunted the female experts—the midwives and mothers and meddlesome-if-handy neighbors—to the side. The costumes had the side benefit of allowing Smellie to smuggle in tools, such as forceps.

Every fact of Smellie seems positively Shakespearean, a comedy of errors: from the costumes and identity confusion to his absurd name. A subtle villainy, violating these mothers too engrossed in their own pain to notice what was hidden underneath his shoddy disguises. The mothers assumed safety at the hands of other women, women who understood their bodies and needs and brought with them millennia of accumulated wisdom. They hadn't consented to male interference nor to the strange and frightening instruments he wanted to try out on their bodies. In this way Smellie smacks more of Shakespearean tragedy, one of the early acts, before the play's death toll has begun to mount but hinting at the bloodier bits to come.

Hello baby, I say to the boy in the blue cap. *They tell me you are mine and I am yours. This is how it will be from now on.* He cries out as though in pain and I open my eyes to the blank containment-room walls and my in-laws standing bedside in mismatched clothes, holding Jed as he sobs silently into their shoulders. They have driven straight through from Minnesota. Their footsteps roused me, not my baby's cry, because he is born but cannot cry (ventilator, stupor) and lies many floors away in a place where, even if he could cry, I wouldn't hear him.

My in-laws have brought donuts, purchased down the street at a place with a pink and white striped awning I know from a previous life, and we offer one to the efficient and tight-lipped postpartum nurse when she brings in the paper cup of pain pills. Maybe kindness can save us from fate. It's a prayer, this donut, a sacrifice placed at the feet of a stone idol.

No, she says, *not right now, I just ate, but thank you very much. That's kind of you.*

The idol moves: Checks my blood pressure, tucks hair behind her ear, adjusts the bag of fluids, removes the full pouch of urine from the end of the catheter, attaches an empty one, hands me the cup of pills, watches as I swish the capsules down, scans the barcode into the records for insurance. Someone has to get paid at the end of all this.

Are you sure? my mother-in-law asks. She holds up the donut box.

The nurse relents, turns backs, takes one. *Thank you,* she says. She leaves. Maybe she throws the donut away in the hallway.

It doesn't matter. She took it.

The need for symbolism is not subsumed by the extremity of circumstance; if anything, it's heightened. This impulse forms the crux of religious yearning—the urge to see deeper meaning in life, especially in catastrophes (the temple destructions and floods and cities leveled as women turned to pillars of salt). Symbolism wears down; the object and symbol tighten until they collapse. The flood becomes redemption, is no longer about the water, per se; the nurse becomes an idol, her skin hardening to stone. In literary terms, this is called metonym. I hadn't realized that the splitting of self from the body turns the entire world into metonym. Nothing's fully real, and so it's all symbol.

William Smellie sometimes demonstrated his methods on destitute mothers, but more often he resorted to the use of an elaborate doll mother and baby made of wood and leather, beer filling a model bladder. Students would pay to observe his lessons. Whether the women and children were real or artificial didn't much matter, as long as the pupils could accumulate enough of the tutorials to ply their trade. The epidural relieved my pain, but it turned me into a doll, a floppy thing that could be acted upon. Probably this made it easier for the doctors as they crowded around, and easier now for the nurse as she tends to wounds I can't fully feel. I also can't feel the urine, tinted beer-yellow, as it leaves me and accumulates in the bag.

I want to ask the phlebotomist and nurse tech and the man who brings food on a tray that I don't eat and the lactation consultant who mistakenly checks on us before realizing her error and backs away and the woman who empties the blue trash can filled with soaked sanitary pads and empty cups: what happens to culpability when error isn't accidental or subconscious but is more removed—an automatic process of blood and vessels and muscles gone awry? And how can an opening, a beginning, involve such total collapse and flattening? It's like my life has suddenly turned into a series of riddles I can't crack.

Every hour the tightlipped donut nurse enters the seal of our containment room to check my reflexes. She needs to ensure my disease and its treatment haven't overtaken my neurological instincts. *Sleep,* she says, when she leaves, as though the hour between mandated checks is enough time to rest. Should I tell her about the magnesium-induced voices that still take over when I close my eyes?

When doctors began to usurp the power of midwives, they did so under the guise of professionalism and safety. They thought they could bring a new rigor to the field, like the procedural checks the nurse performs on me at designated intervals. They imbued their work with a formality they assumed only men could impart. As they took over, the field became so obsessed with preserving women's modesty that physicians conducted exams while looking away, the body in question obscured by cloth. Often the women would lie facing away from the doctors; avoiding eye contact was paramount. Students were forbidden to train on actual deliveries; they learned entirely from textbooks and sketches. Often, the first time they saw a birth, they were in charge of it. For whose benefit was all of this hiding?

My baby's birth was likely one of the first attended by the hospital's new crop of residents, recent med school grads just welcomed to the unit, who gathered around in a huddle while Dr. G. used the forceps to extract the limp baby. I was an instructional tool, a living PowerPoint presentation or a CPR dummy or a Smellian doll. I wore a gown, but the material imparted a sense of modesty without actually covering anything. This kind of practical instruction is likely a good thing, in the aggregate, for medical education—better a human doll than a wooden one—and yet it was strange to be converted into a prop.

The cloaked white patients of early male doctors were the recipients of a relatively decent form of paternalism; their bodies were at least treated with a kind of strange, over-the-top reverence. Not so the bodies of enslaved women, who became living laboratories for a system built on denying their humanity and agency. About a century after the costumed intrusions of William Smellie, Alabama doctor Marion J. Sims performed a series of excruciating experimental gynecologic surgeries—over and over again on the same handful of women—without the aid of anesthetics. Dr. Sims bargained for access to their bodies as a part of a deal with plantation owners: They would hand over the women and in return would get more labor (if he could fix their fistulas, Sims argued, the women could both work again and bear more children); Sims would benefit via clout and elevated standing in the field; white women on the sidelines would receive better care as a result of his breakthroughs. The enslaved women themselves got no choice in the matter, but their unfathomable pain—a far cry from the tidy Victorian ideal of pain doled out in just the right amount—was the primary currency of the entire exchange.

This was an infinitely crueler, cruder version of the capitalism I felt rushing toward me in the packed aisles of BuyBuy Baby, and in the postpartum room with sparkling lake views touted on the hospital tour. Parenting and healthcare today take up residence in a more palatable version of the profit-over-people structure—slick hospital billboards dotting the city, medical notes and diagnostic codes sent to insurance companies who will later charge us co-pays and deductibles for the privilege of having a baby frozen in stasis. Only some people don't get insurance coverage or the choice of the premier hospital advertising its gold stars. Plantations may be reimagined as oak-canopied wedding venues, but are the guests sampling hors d'oeuvres or sipping champagne in the very spot where Dr. Sims' (until recently, known as the "father of modern gynecology") blood-soaked operating table once sat? The past presses down, never far. It's easier to look away from it, but it will never leave.

Throughout the night, different nurses rotate through my room, all preaching a principle of pain management: if not kept in check, pain feeds on itself, metastasizing until medications no longer dampen it. They look to Jed, male figure of reason, as if he's the key to convincing me of this fundamental truth. His face remains vacant. *Even if you think you're feeling better, keep taking the meds,* they say, but they're addressing him and not me.

Pain advice connects to a larger motto: *You can't care for your baby if you don't care for yourself.* Selfishness in guise of selflessness, or maybe vice versa. But I'm not caring for my baby. The hospital is. He's not really mine, so the warning rings false.

With the male takeover of maternity care, mortality rates rose. Doctors, unlike midwives, took on a wide range of duties, including treating patients with contagious diseases and performing autopsies. There was no such thing as germ theory. They might go from a festering wound or decaying corpse to a delivery, sticking their unwashed hands inside the birth canal. Medical history is riddled with cases of doctors and so-called cures doing more harm than good. The modern emphasis on schedules and protocol, on taking medications at the indicated time, is a bulwark against this; if care is systematized it can prevent catastrophe. It's also a way to turn care into a business, to streamline profits and prevent lawsuits. But I've seen the ways catastrophe sneaks in around the edges when it wants to, when it's determined enough.

Don't let her skip a dose, a nurse tells Jed in the middle of the night. He nods, makes his face look serious to indicate compliance, squeezes my hand. He's still on my side. The nurse echoes the warning that haunted me the day before, but in another era, of mothers, naïve and overeager, arriving too early at triage only to be sent home to wait for real labor. Women who did not understand their bodies and misinterpreted their pain. The nurse points to the whiteboard, where we are supposed to be keeping meticulous track of doses. We haven't been. *Set an alarm on your phone for each one,* she commands. Schedules and machines know better than women when it's time.

Dr. Sims tried to justify the pain he inflicted with each surgery with the assumption that it must be welcomed, because it held the promise of fixing a disabling injury. Did he dare to imagine the way that kind of pain manifests in the body, burrowing deep down in the psyche? That pain is not a one and done proposition, but something that lingers and recurs, bobbing up and down on the surface of the water. That the promised cure, and its attendant denial of any agency, might be worse than the sickness. Pain does not make a woman more of a woman, contrary to the opinions of so many throughout so much of time. And anyway, it's questionable if Dr. Sims considered the enslaved women capable of approaching this ideal version of woman. In order to inflict cruelty of that magnitude, in order to trade on their pain, he had to cordon them off, outside the realm of "woman." They were women only insofar as their physiology could be generalized; what he learned on them could be taken and applied to white women. In his eyes, they were akin to Smellie's wooden and leather mannequins.

Today, hospitals provide blood transfusions to treat postpartum hemorrhage, antibiotics for infection, sterile surgery to deliver too-large or too-stuck babies. My belief in the goodness of this progress gave me a false sense of security. Without knowing it, I put my faith in the male order, in the structures that followed from paternalistic takeover. Nothing bad could happen to me because birth was modern and medicalized.

It was also my whiteness that allowed me to approach delivery without skepticism, leading me to believe that obstetrics, and all its prongs descended from Sims, naturally had my best interests at heart. I was one of a long chain of white women turning their heads away from the screams of the enslaved women writhing in the operating theater. Unaware of this history and so, in my own way ignoring their pain, I could regard scientific progress as, ultimately, beneficent, a force for good. In this way I wore my whiteness like a gossamer cloak—so light and airy I hardly felt it against me.

Now, shoved in the containment room, all the cloaks I wore without knowing it when I entered the double doors of triage, the assumptions I carried with me through the years, have been torn off; the things that once felt safe and sure are no longer. When I shake, the nurses tell me it's the waves of postpartum hormones washing through me and that it's normal, but it also may be that my skin is suddenly exposed, and I can feel the claustrophobic closeness of the past I thought was farther away brushing up against me. I'm not so modern after all.

How are you feeling? the donut nurse asks, back again for the day shift. I wonder about the donut, if she savored it, slowly chewing each bite at the nurse's station, or if she ate it in a few large bites, scurrying between her other patient rooms. She seems somehow softer, kinder. *Are the meds working?*

It's strange, I tell her, *to mourn someone living. Whose eyes I haven't seen.* She smiles, opens the shades. Has she heard me?

There, she says. *That's better. These rooms can be so gloomy.*

You could have a Fourth of July baby, our photographer friend said. *That would be fun.* We were sitting on the rooftop of our new apartment with an almost unbroken view of the Chicago skyline. *You can bring it up here to watch the fireworks.*

If the baby's on time, I said. *If we're home by then.*

Our friend took pictures of me and Jed against the backdrop of the city so we could document this moment before arrival. We felt lucky. Here we were, floating above the street, perfect pregnancy, perfect baby squirming beneath my blue shirt. The Sears Tower soared behind us, vast lake in the distance, stretching and stretching, beyond the scope of the camera's lens.

We ate takeout fried chicken and coleslaw and macaroni with flimsy plastic forks and everyone except me sipped beers and someone told the story of his wife, stuck in a hospital bed in preterm labor, cervix sewn shut. (The baby was, in the end, born at term and healthy.)

Cervical cerclage: when a doctor sews a woman shut to keep the baby in. It sounds lilting, poetic. The medical term for the body part requiring said procedure: incompetent cervix. The organ as delinquent, distracted, too self-absorbed to perform the assigned maternal task, I thought then, hand on my protruding abdomen. Clearly a term devised by a man.

Now my medical records contain similar phrasing. My pelvis is deemed "adequate," and my "expulsive effort" "good" as though my body was graded for its performance. It reeks of the Victorian, the idea of a paragon of a woman who feels just the right amount of pain.

The language of medicine alters how practitioners and patients alike experience its reality, and who they regard as protagonists. Dr. Sims devised a speculum known, until recently, as "The Sims." Kameelah Phillips, a contemporary Black physician, decided to rechristen it "The Lucy," in honor of an enslaved woman forced to undergo Sims' surgical experimentation. Finally, one of them gets included in the transactional chain, but it's too little too late. The patient herself isn't around to reap the benefits. Renaming is a protective measure, warning contemporary women and doctors of the injustices of the past in the hopes that we'll be wiser and more humane, but it's not restorative. Lucy doesn't get to know about the renaming, about the attempts to honor her memory. My childhood rabbi might wave this away and say that we live on in memory, but the adult, less meek version of me would correct him—*No, memory is memory and life is life.* Lucy is dead, and so this memorial cannot reach her, not where she is now. The memory is for the rest of us.

Centuries after the Chamberlen brothers and William Smellie and their prodding tools and all the men following in their footsteps who claimed to know better than women, the natural birthing movement arose as a course correction to combat birth's medicalization. But it sometimes went too far, dangerously arguing for pain as virtue, as *the* thing that would make a woman a woman and allow her to fulfill her maternal destiny, for intervention as superfluous, forgetting that a flawed process of modernization had brought with it much positive change. Besides, often it was male doctors, like the ones who had originally seized power, positioning themselves as the experts on women's bodies. History repeats itself. Men put on a new disguise as the champions of natural womanhood, but underneath, their message—an intrusive "doctor knows best"—was made of the same stuff as it was hundreds of years before.

Grantly Dick-Read of *Childbirth Without Fear* scorns the type of woman who stubbornly resists instruction to relax in the face of fear and pain: *Women who do not want their babies, who are bored by the whole procedure, and who feel they are merely doing a duty and are fed up at having to do it.* His vision of women's empowerment via pain comes at a steep cost. In his paradigm, women assume responsibility for the outcome, good or bad. Their inability to accept their pain and calm their bodies might constrict the birth canal, impeding the baby's safe passage.

Would Dr. Dick-Read think this was the cause of my baby's predicament, stuck now in his icy blue cap? Would he have looked at me, balancing on that ball in the delivery room, requesting the anesthesiologist for the epidural (because at a mere four centimeters the contractions were already too much to bear) and shaken his head, muttering *Well this can't bode well?* Would he have thought: *If only she had managed without pain relief, she might have felt the tightening inside, the flow narrowing. She might have been able to relax her muscles and set the baby free?*

During pregnancy I couldn't help but absorb the warnings of these mid-century men. Their theories were propagated by the doula in the coffee shop, the woman I bought the dining table from, the yoga instructor in the studio below my apartment. I didn't know their names but I heard their message loud and clear. The men had receded but not before becoming part of the prenatal landscape.

The alarm on Jed's phone goes off. It's time to pump. He's set it for every two hours, marking off the sessions on the whiteboard. Sometimes when it rings it signifies time to pump, sometimes it means I need to take ibuprofen or acetaminophen. As a controlled substance, Norco administration remains the nurses' responsibility, so that's removed from our list of duties. Jed tracks which alarms are for meds and which are for pumping and which are for both.

So far all I've been able to extract is nothing or rusty pipe, neither of which can be saved in the NICU freezer for the baby once he defrosts. *You don't have to do this,* Jed says. *Really.* He wants me to sleep in the allotted minutes between disturbances, though I'm not sleeping, more like shutting my eyes and listening to the rogue magnesium voices and trying to determine what they have to tell me. The voices utter things in the shape of words but without any sense. The closer I listen the more they crumble.

But I do, I tell him. He pulls the pump bedside. I begin to assemble the plastic parts. It's the only way I can see to try to seize back control, to make up for my body's betrayal. I haven't read Dr. Dick-Read but I'm groveling at the feet of men like him, feeling the hot poke of shame, trying to atone for where I've gone off-course.

I switch on the machine but there's no suction. The instructions included with the parts tell me I've forgotten to attach the small, soft piece that forms a seal at the top of the bottle, flapping back and forth like a tongue. The manual knows better than me, the supposed mother who's incapable of correctly operating a simulacrum of her body, let alone the actual thing.

Wild West

At some point the midwife and a frontier newcomer—mail-order wife to the jailkeeper—come to the shed. I do not know how long it's been since I was deposited here because, as I am discovering, a ghost loses track of time. It's irrelevant when it stretches out before you, unending. A vestment worn into a shapeless fabric. Because I don't know how much time has passed, I'm not lonely. Loneliness depends on time. But still, I am glad for their company.

The two women kneel over my empty body like penitents, dipping rags in buckets of dirty water, and gently cleanse the blood and muck from the insides of my thighs. It has caked on thick. Does this mean it's been days that I've been dead? There is something like love to their gentleness, though of course I can't feel it, floating above. I try to remember the way my husband would stroke the back of my neck and run his fingers through my hair, but the very notion of touch escapes me. With a sponge, the jailer's wife tries to clean the hair down below but only succeeds in spreading dirty liquid, now more blood and guts than water, around the matted mess.

The women dip and dip and rub and rub and rub until the skin begins to crack from the friction. My body is like one of those chickens I would buy whole at market, then pluck and clean. The ankles and calves are swollen, and fluid stagnates around the joints. The jailer's wife dabs her index finger at the bottom lip, swollen where I bit down in the throes of pains and broke the skin, then smooths a palm across my forehead and cheeks. I hardly knew her, had spoken mere words to her when I was living, but her touch, I can tell, is tender and kind.

Poor thing, the jailer's wife says.

Hush. None of that. The midwife chastens. *She's at peace. With the Lord and her babe.*

Probably, though, she thinks me damned for eternity.

It's not as simple as you think, I want to tell her, about the afterlife, which is so far marked by the absence of boundaries, a porousness that is neither good nor bad. It's not salvation or damnation, heaven or hell. Not the things her husband spends his life preaching. It's floating and suspension.

Did the babe have a name? the jailer's wife asks.

The midwife sucks her lips in and shakes her head. *Died before it was born.*

Oh, says the jailer's wife. *Shame. Wanted to know so I could say a prayer for the little lamb, but I'd need a name. How else would God know who the prayer's for?*

The midwife doesn't have an answer, which I find strange since she's married to the preacher. Shouldn't there be another way for an almighty God to know who prayers are meant for? But it doesn't matter. Here I am, floating in this timelessness and there is no God, not as far as I can see. Or perhaps the wide expanse of time and space is God. The preacher has gotten it all wrong.

The jailer's wife takes a metal comb from her pocket and pulls it through the hair. It catches at once, the tangled curls unyielding, but she keeps at it, hacking away at snarls until one knot loosens and another. When she's done what she can, she lifts the head onto her knee, pulls the mess back and ties it with a piece of twine. *Better than cutting it off,* she explains, though the midwife has not questioned her. *Some dignity in it.*

The midwife rolls my body to one side, same as she had in the midst of the pains. While she holds it in place, the jailer's wife unfastens the soiled dress and together they yank it down. It catches on the hips. *Not too fast,* the preacher's wife warns. The body's bones shift and crackle as they snake through the fabric.

The women tending to the body grow hungry; perhaps it is afternoon. I can almost remember what afternoon feels like, the hot glow of sun low in the sky, the way I'd squint in the clearing. They unwrap bread from handkerchiefs and, with a knife, pare slices of meat from a marbled slab. They take big bites, gnaw the provisions in one cheek and then the other. They are too busy eating to talk and the only sound is of chewing, like cows. The body sits naked. I try to imagine hunger but I can't remember the feeling of it in my gut, not quite. Hunger is reserved for the living. A great many things are reserved for the living.

When they are done, they spread a clean dress out in the hay. It's a simple one, cornflower blue, that I sewed when I first arrived out west. I had to leave most of my wardrobe behind for the journey. Only so much can fit in a single trunk. Now the two wives cut the back open with their knife, gristle from their lunch meat still lacing some of the teeth, and slip it onto one arm and the other. It takes much effort because the body's arms and neck flop and sag. They pull the fabric over the belly, swollen where the emptied womb floats like one of those pig-bladder balloons the children toss back and forth, take a sash and tie it around the waist to hold the dress in place. In another world, that belly could still be full with child.

Once the dress is in place they button the neck all the way to the chin. They want to defend the body's modesty, even in death. It doesn't matter that no one will see the body when it's arrayed in a coffin, which I hear them say my husband is building with lumber left over from the construction of our cabin.

The two wives gather their rags and combs and knives, the dirty dress. They dump the black water remaining in their pail into the hay beside the body, and tiptoe out as though afraid they might disturb me. My blue dress rustles in the wind that makes its way in through the gap where the bottom of the door does not touch the ground. Flies begin to nestle in my body's crevices.

In the dark, men I don't recognize come to the shed to fetch the body. They bring with them a rough-hewn coffin situated in the bed of a horse-drawn wagon, much like the one that took me out west in the first place, brought me far from home. They lift my body up and over the lip of the box and close the top with a thud and raise the whole thing up and up and bring down the whip on the flexed back of the horse. From above I scan the faces for my husband, in case I missed him the first time around, but he isn't there.

Without good reason to stay with the body, I float away. I hover over to the doctor's cabin—his home and also where he administers salves and elixirs—which sits on the edge of town beside a henhouse. The trapped birds cluck and flap their wings. Feathers swirl.

Inside, the doctor stands over his examination table and pulls the bundle he took from the midwife, wrapped like a lopsided loaf of bread, from his satchel. His hands are fat and sloppy and he almost drops the small thing, still layered in the waxy white that coated it in the womb, as he unravels the paper, but manages to catch it on his protruding belly. His thumbs falter and grasp the slick of the thin forearms. I feel the urge to scream but have nothing with which to emit the sound. I want to reach for the baby's head but have no arms and no sense of how much space separates me from him.

The doctor takes a scalpel and slices the baby down the middle with one quick motion. He reaches into the chest and extracts the miniature organs. He holds each one up to the lamp and turns them over and over again. The heart, one lung and the other, the stomach. He closes his eyes and feels the membranes with his thumbs. He spits a chew of tobacco out onto the dirt floor, then adjusts the position of his oil lamp and examines again, this time with his magnifying glass. He holds the parts up under his nose and sniffs. When he is done with them, he stuffs them back inside the skin, jumbled in the gaping cavity, then stitches the torso shut with coarse black thread. He seems in a rush.

Then he fetches his saw from a hook on the back wall. He holds the blade high above his head, lowers it slowly to the scalp. He holds it between the eyebrows. He is still. I see a shiver run up his body and he begins to push the blade against the skin, thin and papery, and then into the skull below. The sound is wretched. This is what he really wants, I can tell. What preceded was him going through the motions to get to this point. Small fragments of bone crumble onto the table. He continues to saw back and forth.

He takes the sides of the skull and separates them with his hands as though pulling apart a large fruit. He removes the insides and holds up the brain—wet, slippery creature—squints to better discern the ridges and folds. He sits there, frozen, brain held high. He whistles, long and victorious.

Later he places the brain in a jar, floating amidst yellow liquid. He puts it on the shelf beside his bed, between an amputated hand and a lesioned liver. He shakes his head. No, that will not do. He takes the hand and liver and puts them on the floor below. Now the brain sits alone, higher than anything else in the room.

Did it hurt? I ask the baby, or what remains of it, there on the table.

Do I mean his death inside me or the doctor's sawing? I'm not sure, perhaps both.

He doesn't answer. I consider what the jailer's wife said, about the baby needing a name for prayer. Does he need a name for me, so I can call to him, so he can respond? It's too late, though, because a ghost cannot name. I remember the concept of a name from when I was alive but cannot remember any specific names, not the name of my husband or my mother or my name, much less the names I had considered for this now-dissected creature back when my stomach was still full, not with bloat but with baby.

Chicago

Someone knocks, opens the first door and then the second, enters the containment room. *Time to choose a name*, a woman says, with a broad smile. She's gripping a clipboard, pulls off the top sheet. The form's bureaucratic type reads, "Certificate of Live Birth."

The baby is so far away and the magnesium voices are so insistent, a constant thrum in the background, that I've forgotten we need to pick a name.

You put your names here, the woman says, pointing to a line, *and your address here. Then the baby's name here. It's simple. The hospital completes the rest.* She hands the form to Jed, along with a pen. He places it down on the table without looking. *I'll be back later to pick it up,* she says. *Take your time.*

I want to ask: is this the right form for our baby? For our situation? Because my son—he wasn't born fully alive. He had a heartbeat but wasn't breathing. Does that count? Is that alive or dead?

I would ask my questions but have learned answers don't matter. There are only half-answers leading to more questions. There is: *We aren't sure yet* or *We have to wait and see* or *We don't yet fully understand.*

Stuck in the containment room, we are butting up against the limits of knowledge, ones we always knew existed but never felt with our own fingertips. We are being spat out like a tidal wave against a concrete wall, pulled back to sea, spat back out again.

There is no land as far as we can see.

The opposite of live birth isn't dead birth but stillbirth, connotative of still life: objects posed on canvas, soft light filtered through a window. Sometimes there's a rabbit hung upside down, ready to be skinned. Before I became a woman of this hospital, I went to grad school across the street from an art museum. I'd spend time between classes wandering the galleries, picking a painting at random, sitting on a bench in front of it, and staring, focusing on one particular detail, maybe the way the light reflected off an urn or the arch of a man's brow. What has happened to us: not still life or portraiture, not stillbirth or live birth, but something else without a label, lingering between.

In high school, after I discovered poetry wasn't only concerned with rhyme, I learned prose wasn't only concerned with plot or character. In *Lolita*, my high school writing teacher explained, as though unfurling a secret only he contained deep within his bald, shining head, Vivian Darkbloom was an anagram for Vladimir Nabokov. He said wordplay lent the book a playful air, prioritized nuance of language above all else. *I am not what I seem*, it announced.

If one studied the names in Lolita's class roster, the teacher pointed out, there were an abundance of "Roses" embedded in the list. Is there meaning to the choice, besides delight in discovery of pattern, of secret code between author and attuned reader? Horror of plot washed in beauty of language. Does a wash get it all out?

At some point Jed unearths the bureaucratic form from under our accumulated mess and picks up a pen and with a jot we choose the name Jonah, just like that, because we cannot keep calling him Baby, because he is still the baby of the hospital but we must take steps to make him our baby, even if we don't believe it to be true or if I'm not sure I want it to be true. We choose Jonah simply because it is a name we always liked, one we scribbled on our list months ago in the happy flurry of baby preparations. We are too exhausted to think more deeply.

Only later do we realize the symbolic significance of biblical Jonah, a prophet in mortal danger deep inside the belly of the whale before being spit onto dry land, even if that land is only Ninevah, ungodly den of sin. The name Jonah, we learn, means dove, which also recalls the story of the flood, forty days and forty nights, the bird who summoned back land from beneath fifteen cubits of water. We choose Chaim as the middle name because the bald chaplain who lingered uncomfortably near the door of our room told us sick adults traditionally added this name, Hebrew for *life*, as a plea for healing, a last-ditch attempt to ward off the angel of death. Our ancestors, weathered and stooped, quaking with some fever that has swept across the shtetl's snowy tin roofs. This name was a prayer thrown at a god who no longer intervened.

To name is to lay claim to, and this is what we are doing with the baby who is far away on another floor. In Hebrew, a person's name is completed by the phrase *son/daughter of____*. Doctors too stake out their territory in this way. Take, for example, procedures for freeing babies stuck on their way through their mother's birth canals. A hand trapped at the side of the face or a shoulder nestled too comfortably in the pelvis can be released with a push here or a knee there. One imagines that centuries ago some grandmother or weathered neighbor executed the same trick out of instinct, out of necessity—skills passed down from generation to generation. No matter. Now they are the McRoberts Maneuver, Mauriceau-Smellie-Viet Maneuver, Lovset Manuever, Rubin Maneuver. The women of the past have been shoveled out of the way and forgotten. In choosing Jonah's name we are shoveling other potential versions of our child out of the way. Already a prior version of him was swept away without my awareness; I'll never know the baby he was before the injury, and now I'll never know the other versions of him that could have been, under other names. With each action, intentional and not, the pathway narrows.

You have to trick your body into thinking the baby is hungry, the nurses (NICU, postpartum, dayshift, night) tell me, so it will produce milk. *It's a supply and demand system*, they repeat. We are an economy, not a family. They will stash my dregs in a NICU freezer labeled with name and date, where they will wait until/if the baby can eat by mouth, if/when his suck and swallow reflex emerges from the muck. We are not only an economy but also a conditional program. We are many things before we are a family. At least I have named him, I think. At least I have done this one thing to claim him. That gets us one step closer, perhaps, to family, though I'm still not sure that's what I want.

I try to trick my body into thinking the pump is my baby and I also try to trick my baby into thinking I'm his mother. The NICU nurses have given me small pieces of heart-shaped felt to put in my bra. This way, they say, my smell will transfer to the fabric. I am to bring these back with me on each visit and they will place the hearts next to Jonah's head as a comfort and a sort of early, subliminal lesson in attachment. It's all subterfuge.

I pump and pump and still the milk doesn't excrete. *It's hard,* the nurses say, *without an actual baby's mouth to stimulate production.* They are attempting to express compassion. I am attempting to express milk. Express is the name, I learn, for when something other than the baby pulls milk out of a breast. *The pump mimics but isn't the same, you know?*

I nod, but do not know.

You could pump more often, nurses suggest. *See if that helps.* They call this power pumping, like some kind of cultish workout class. It imitates the newborn baby's unremitting hunger, cluster feeding, apparently common a day after birth when the baby has shaken off the exhaustion of delivery and wakes enough to realize it's ravenous. My baby is doing no such thing but my body, apparently, should be primed for this phenomenon anyway. My body should be on motherhood autopilot, driven by hormones, but the looming dread I feel, and my ambivalence about motherhood, about claiming the baby of the hospital as mine, may be interfering. One nurse suggests brown bread and dark ale when I get home. Another tells me to take fenugreek capsules and drink anise tea. *Most of all,* they admonish, *relax, relax, relax. Stress impacts supply.*

While traditional Jewish practice denied a stillborn baby official religious mourning rites, trying to cushion the blow of the loss, those infants were still bestowed with names. Names were tethers, allowing parents to find the child in the next world. The world to come apparently filled with panicked mothers yelling the names of their long-lost babies out into an abyss. Maybe what I'm doing now is a version of that, writing his name on the blank line and hoping he hears me floors away. He's lost in his blue cap and I need to find him.

That was delicious, the postpartum nurse says, referring to the donut. She's back on for this shift. She writes "Jonah" in bubbly script on the whiteboard, next to my name and Jed's. She brushes her hands together, pleased with the progress we've made. Jed is half asleep on the couch. A beam of sunlight hits his forehead like it's a slab of ham or cheese in a still-life painting. The two of us are shells of our former selves and the baby is a jot of dry-erase marker. This is nothing like the transformation into a family of three I envisioned when I foresaw the postnatal pictures I would take with the camera I had my friend bring with our go-bag. The nurse's rubber shoes squeal out of the room.

Information passes through me; nothing sticks. I forget what floor I'm on and what floor Jonah is on. We make the trip back and forth, back and forth, back and forth, Jed pushing my wheelchair. I am not allowed to go on my own, am not allowed to walk because of the magnesium, but, even if I were, I would lose my way. Each time we board the elevator I can't remember if I should press the up or down button. I've never had a reliable sense of direction. Learning to drive as a teenager, I would find myself in strange parts of New Orleans—the city I'd been born and raised in but somehow could not navigate—spat off the wrong highway exit without my knowledge and suddenly steering down a narrow bridge over a swamp.

In Mother/Baby Suite 1089B there are more knocks, what the nurses continue to refer to as suspected seizures, but I strain to believe them—to me the movements still look like evidence of life. There's nothing else to cling to. The baby has no more information to give us about his prognosis. He's in a state of suspended animation.

The baby, I try to remind myself, is now Jonah. He has a name. This should begin to make him mine, to convert me into a mother.

As I wait for the name to begin to have its intended effect, I reach out to the baby and place two fingers on his small ankle the way the gentle nurse has instructed us, so as not to cause him more pain or raise his body temperature above the set threshold. He is so soft, so vulnerable. I want to keep my hand there and this might be—maybe, just maybe—the beginnings of motherhood erupting.

Jonah, Jonah, Jonah, I subvocalize in the hallway on the way to visit him. I'm practicing.

The Jewish god is so abstract the name stays hidden, out of earshot. We're given substitutes for use in prayer but none of them are god's actual name. God can be "Elohim," the etymologically plural form of god that derives from Judaism's pagan cousins, or "YHVH," also known as the tetrammagaton, which, lacking vowels or oral history (superstition meant the word went unspoken) is unpronounceable, or "Adonai," which means "lord" and isn't supposed to be spoken except in prayer; saying it in the wrong context desecrates it. In its place, religious Jews use "HaShem," which simply translates as "The Name." This emphasis on naming, or rather on obscuring the ultimate name, imbues names with a metonymic power. The name becomes the thing it references, and so, with a figure like god, it's important to tread carefully around the name, just as one needs to tread carefully around god. I too have to tread carefully around the name we've chosen. If I say the name "Jonah," I will be referring not to the baby of the hospital, but to my baby. I will be the mother. Is this a step I'm willing to take? Continuing to think of him as "the baby" is my way of keeping him abstract; "the baby" is the HaShem of the hospital. He's a blank slate. He might be anything and belong to anyone. I might be free to go.

I don't ask anyone if the baby will survive. The thick blue tube in his mouth breathes for him: in/out, in/out. Doctors explain that he'll stay three days frozen in this stasis: blue cap, blue tube, body still except for occasional rattle of seizures, which lend him the eerie trappings of liveliness, none of its substance.

We'll know more after three days, they say, referring to the cooling cap protocol. The three repeats and repeats until it expands to fill all the space: the Mother/Baby Suite and the containment room and all the bathrooms and waiting rooms and nurses' stations and halls and elevators between us, and the triage unit downstairs by the entrance with the singing doorman. There's so much of it, bulky presence of these days, blocking me, locking me in, that I forget there's outside. There's only me and Jed and the soft baby whose eyes remain swollen shut, who is still not fully our baby, though we have given him a name and wear bracelets that rub our wrists, linking us to him, and these three days. I don't know if I am afraid of the possibility of his death or the alternative and this is what sits at the heart of my hesitation to speak his actual name, his given name.

When he stops by Jonah's bedside, Dr. R. points to clues that might indicate the severity of his state: his seizures are a foreboding prognostic sign, but lack of secondary organ damage, which they have determined by weighing diapers to evaluate kidney function and examining his heart and lungs, is good. His initial brainwave activity gathered prior to the cap is a positive, but his blood gases—evidence of excess buildup of acid, like he's some toxic waste site—a negative. Nothing definite can be determined.

The origins of his state lie similarly shrouded. What to trace Jonah's predicament back to? Is it possible to trace it at all? Could it be infection? Failed placenta? Cord compression? I would like a label for what happened, but the doctors intimate that they may never find one. Still, they send samples of things out for testing, grow cultures in the lab, conduct spinal taps. *Probably inconclusive,* they tell me. They don't expect to get an answer, and they don't want me to expect one, either.

The pediatric neurologist also visits, though there's not much he can do or say while we wait for the three days to go by. He wears a Hawaiian shirt with big pink flowers bursting open, Georgia O'Keefe style. *He always wears Hawaiian shirts,* the NICU nurse tells us. *It's his thing.* I didn't know neurologists had things. He's stout with a thick, gray beard—a tropical Santa. *Sometimes things just happen*, he says, by way of justifying why we are here in the NICU talking to him. *Sometimes there's no explanation. It's a black box*, he says, referring to my womb. My father-in-law continually mispronounces the neurologist's name no matter how many times we correct him, perhaps a way of undercutting his authority so that later, whatever prognoses this doctor trots out, we won't have to believe them.

Psychologist Erik Erikson built on Freud's ideas to try to understand human development over an entire lifespan. Erikson emerged from his own sort of black box; he was self-made, self-created. His given name was Erik Homberger. The Erikson he added in adulthood, once he began to establish himself as a pillar of the psychological community. Erik, son of Erik, though his father's name wasn't Erik but Theodor. Or at least Theodor was his stepfather's name; no one knew the identity of his biological father. His mother must have known, but her story is unrecorded. Erikson's name was an adopted self; name as costume; name as self-reflexive stunt; name as lie.

Jonah's name, newly bestowed, is also a kind of stunt. We're tricking the world into thinking we're parents. We're tricking ourselves. We are going through the motions of parenting but the steps are hollowed out. We're putting our faith in the power of the name to become something more. It's a version of fake it 'til you make it. We hope the name will transform into a container of meaning, create a path for our son and, by extension, for us, just as Erikson's name did for him. But for now, the name "Jonah" is a random collection of letters, of sounds. In my head I say it over and over again trying to make it become more real, but, like any quotidian word—blanket or carpool—repeated too many times, it only becomes stranger; eventually the signifier unhinges from the signified.

Meanwhile, Jonah's blue cap freezes time with its flow of chilled liquid, which cools his blood before it pulses from heart to lungs and back to his head, giving neurons a chance to shake off brittle ends. We freeze alongside him, wait three days, the number a magical incantation, a prayer. After three days, the doctors say, we will remove the cap. After three days, they say, we will assess brain function. After three days, we will get an MRI. After three days we will understand something of the moment of tightening that occurred deep inside me, undetected—not so long ago but also in another era, part of an alternative historical progression. We traveled one path and the road veered and took us with it. A Robert Frost poem of labor.

After three days, they say, they will hazard a guess about what lies in store for the baby. *A guess*, the Hawaiian-shirted neurologist emphasizes, trying to prepare us for answers that aren't answers regarding a baby who is not fully our baby. More black boxes await. No one explicitly says his future will be our future, too, because that's assumed. I remind myself of this, over and over.

Before I entered this hospital, my future depended on no one else, and, without a reminder, I risk forgetting that my fate hinges on another's. Biblical Jonah flees God and boards a ship to escape. God sends a storm after the boat in retribution, and the other sailors, caught in the upheaval, toss Jonah overboard into the belly of the whale. With Jonah gone, the storms subside and the sea calms. The sailors are saved. They manage to unhinge their fates from Jonah's. But here, with this new Jonah, that kind of unhinging is not possible.

The three days are a grim countdown to our verdict, but also a reprieve from knowledge. I want to stay inside them, fortressed, ensconced, gripping the thread of a belief, thinning each minute as our countdown approaches zero, that the doctors are wrong. Jonah couldn't have been injured, his blood supply couldn't have been severed, because we'd have known. Catastrophes aren't silent and undetectable; they rupture and explode. The MRI image—cortical strands and folds all pulsing beautifully with blood, healthy and plump and glistening—will show them.

During his three days and nights inside the heaving body of the great whale, Biblical Jonah says to God, "from the belly of sheol I cried out/ And You heard my voice." But God hasn't saved him. Not yet. Jonah anticipates redemption as though he's preemptively read to the end of his own book. Our Jonah, per medical protocol, must spend his allotted three days and three nights in a blue cooling cap, knocking on his invisible door, waiting to be let in. We don't get to know what comes next. None of us are prophets and we aren't let in on the future until it happens.

We huddle around the baby, now Jonah, watching his fists knock before the injection of phenobarbital stills them. We move in and out of elevators, from bed to wheelchair and back again, sometimes pausing to look down and watch the unfrozen conduct their lives below. A different species, stretched through the slight curve of window: donning helmets and unlocking bikes, pushing delivery carts out of the backs of trucks, reading books while trying to cross streets, carrying flowers and balloons and babies in and out of doors, shouting into phones at the failures of husbands or mothers or sons. One day will I shout into the phone at the person who the baby in the blue cap will become? Will I say, *Jonah, Jonah can you hear me?* I look down at the pedestrians and try to imagine that I am one of them, going about an ordinary day, wiping sweat from my brow, and that I am calling my son and he responds to his name.

Wild West

I leave the doctor's and glide over Main Street, watching the townsfolk go about their business, the opening and shutting and shuffling and sitting and eating and shitting and butchering and hauling and gambling and bartering and cleaning and burying. The pace is frantic; new structures crop up from dust. In what feels like the span of a single day, a whole street with a rooming house and a leathersmith and tailor emerges in a spoke off the center where the tavern sits. Probably my body is buried at some point while I drift. A ghost does not feel exhaustion, which perhaps accounts for the strangeness of time. Without a body to register fatigue, I have no rhythm, no sense of energy tingling upon waking and diminishing as the sun disappears over the dusty horizon.

From the town, I float to the low hills beside the small settlement of cabins where I once resided. I can make out the very clearing that holds our brown, squat home, the triangular jut of its roof. I am uneasy about revisiting the place where I inhabited a body—where time held itself up as a solid thing that could separate days from nights and one week from the next. I fear it might break something deep within my ghostly self.

If it weren't for the promise I made to my dead child—*I'll find you*—I wouldn't venture so close. I know where his body is, but not the rest of him. There is a chance he might still be there, in our home. Otherwise, I would be far from this place. I seek nothing for myself. I harbor no deep desire to enact my will upon the world left behind.

As I descend, homing in toward the cabin like a mother eagle to her nest, I see my husband pacing in front, hands tucked in the pockets of his vest. His beard is patchy and eyes bloodshot. Too much coffee, I think, imagining him heating the concoction over the open fire, then sipping the thick black sludge from one of our metal cups to stave off sleep, which will now only bring dreams of our life together with our babe and the ensuing despair upon waking to loneliness and the stab of grief.

Oh, how he must miss me! How he must yearn for the days when we were innocent newlyweds, embracing the wide openness of this land, all ours. When we could settle where we wanted and how we wanted. We could create a life from nothing and control its contours completely. Now I know it was all delusion, that sense of control, but while we were staking out our plot of land and gathering materials for building, it felt as real as the ground beneath our feet.

I nestle against the eave above the front door. I remember my husband chopping the wood for the frame, cutting the lumber to the right size, sanding it and nailing the beams together. From my perch I can see the door swing open.

Chicago

Two days after delivery my levels begin to even out. While I was sleeping, nurses spirited away vials of my blood and urine, ferrying them through winding hallways somewhere in the hidden center of the hospital, dropping them behind white doors where hunched-over lab technicians, eyes shielded behind thick plastic goggles, spooled them through machines and examined my cells under microscopes.

The report says the syndrome was indeed cured by expelling the child from my womb. My levels are falling—not normal yet, but trending in the right direction. When one of Dr G.'s associates bounces in to tell me the good news I cry out, a wail I don't feel emerging from my belly or throat but hear pummeling against the bare walls of the room, because it means having to leave this place that has whisked away my child and refuses to let go. I'm still unsure if he is mine, but proximity is the only way to find out.

This is a positive trend. She smiles in a small way that only involves her lips and not her eyes, a way that acknowledges the suffocation of the room, a force qualitatively different from sadness. *Insurance won't cover an inpatient bed if you're bouncing back.* I remember this from birthing class: vaginal deliveries get you two nights in the hospital, c-sections get you four. The hospital was a precious commodity, a chance to recuperate for a handful of nights before returning home to navigate new parenthood alone while also tending to one's own healing body—a daunting task. *Try to deliver after midnight,* the instructor joked, explaining how the clock starts after the baby is born, and all that happened before doesn't count. Couples jotted down notes, like they could somehow game the system.

It'll be good for you to get out, my family says—parents and in-laws and Jed, invisible patient, sleeping on a bed that does not count as a bed and slips silently back into its slot in the wall. My suffocation subsumes his because I am in the real bed tethered to the IV pole with nurses assigned to my care, though his vacant stare bores through the object of focus—the consent form or window or me—searching for something that doesn't exist behind it. Every so often he swipes a hand through his oil-slicked black hair, unwashed now for more days than Jonah has been of the hospital, as though to remind us, to remind himself, he hasn't been washed away.

Everyone must have forgotten that I am as frozen as the baby in the blue cap, the baby I have not yet held, who may or may not be mine. They must have forgotten that the three days are a space as well as a time. The three days are a whale's belly, deep under the sea. We cannot leave. The three days preclude the existence of anything beyond. The three days hold us inside.

Listen to every molecule of your body, whispered the yoga teacher. As though we could break the self down into component parts, turn each piece over in the palms of our heart-clasped hands. As though we could see what was happening inside and control it. We were coming out of one pose, slipping into the next.

The doctor takes a breath and says, *If you want, we can try something.* I haven't asked but she seems to have heard me anyway. She pats the edge of the bed as if to indicate we are friends, collaborators, and pulls out a sheet of paper from under her arm. *Are you in any distress?* she asks.

Yes. (Who wouldn't be?)

Are you having trouble sleeping?

Yes. (Who wouldn't be?)

Do you think it would be dangerous for you to go home?

I know what dark center these questions hurl toward. I wouldn't have the energy to hurt myself–though, for the first time, the end of my life does not terrify me. Only the future I can't see does. I don't tell her this because there's too much noise for nuance.

If we can make the case that you're in too much distress to go home, we can appeal to your insurance to extend your stay. But we'd need documentation. At this point, there's no medical reason to keep you and we'd need to submit a code for coverage.

I have forgotten the distinction between medical and not. Between body and other. I exist in a great mass of undifferentiated matter.

No, I say, gripping the pilled sheet beneath me. *I'm ok. I can leave.* The doctor lets her hand rise slowly off the bed. It hovers for a moment, midair, then plunges to her lap. She doesn't believe me, not completely, but knows her work here is done, that there's nothing more for her to do. Due diligence complete. No way to read a mind. She is letting me go.

I know too much of what happens to patients with SUICIDE RISK tattooed on their medical records. The ink doesn't wash away. Once, when I worked as a research assistant at a university, I met people on the inpatient unit of a psychiatric hospital and watched as they approached the medication window where a nurse would dispense cups of pills and observe the pump of their throats as capsules descended—just as the nurses here watch me swallow pills from paper cups—before allowing them to retreat back to television game shows and plastic couches and small, square windows of thick glass. The patients could see out, but no one could see in. They could watch the street, but they couldn't walk out onto it. Even after discharge, feet firmly on cement, I'm not sure they would fully return to the outside world.

The doctor leaves, feet hitting floor in slow clunks, as though I might change my mind at any moment and she would be forced to turn around. Better to take her time. No one wants to come back into the containment room once they escape.

The nurse, typing something beside the now untethered IV pole, looks up. *I'll go ahead and get your discharge paperwork in order so it's ready when you are.* She extracts herself, too.

I imagine outside air hitting my face as I leave the hospital's sliding doors, hurling me back in, hospital shoving me out again, body in limbo between two worlds that don't want me.

The most difficult segment of labor is transition. The cervix completes its dilation. The body feels itself breaking down the middle.
The woman hovers excruciatingly between incubator and mother. In
Natural Childbirth, Frederick W. Goodrich, Jr. writes, "From four-
fifths to full dilation is the time when you are apt to experience the
most pain in your entire labor. At this time you are apt to become
frustrated, tired, and discouraged." To counter this, he offers guid-
ance, however flimsy ("At this point it is important that you redouble
your efforts to relax") along with a reminder that this too shall pass
("It will probably take about ten more contractions to effect full dilation, at which time you will be in the second stage and you will find
that you feel differently.")

When transition is over, the pushing phase begins. But, like
water breaking, transition does not end. Dr. Goodrich doesn't say
it, but I know. I'm still hovering between incubator and mother.
Leaving the hospital will be another ongoing state as well as a finite
action, just like matter is a wave and a particle at the same time.

You don't have to vacate immediately, the donut nurse says, when she
comes in with the discharge forms for me to sign. It's a small mercy.
The hospital is always offering up bargains of time. Does she remember our offering?

So we stay, squatters, until the cleaning staff makes its way to our
floor, rounds the bend, enters our containment room, plastic waste
bins and mop handles clanking. Our final cue.

It'll be better to get out of here, Jed says, lowering the bedrail to
help me out. He offers his hand. Is he speaking to me or trying to
convince himself? Our bags are packed because we didn't bother to
open them. A laminated checklist on the wall lists the newborn discharge requirements (Hep B vaccine, hearing screen, bath) but none
of it applies.

I have to leave, I tell the baby, on our way out. *I have to go.*

You can call all night long, the NICU nurse tells us. *You can check
in any time.*

When we exit through the doors into the warm air, my in-laws are waiting in the car, parked in the circular driveway at the front of the hospital, beside that beloved doorman in a red vest, the one who sings "Happy Birthday!" to all entering women. This time, to us, he says nothing.

I have to leave, I tell the baby again, looking up at the lines of dark windows where I think the NICU might be. I can't remember the floor.

Jonah's ventilator utters: *I know, I know, I know.*

After his shipmates heave Jonah overboard in order to save themselves, it only takes until the end of the next chapter (which constitutes a handful of lines) before the whale spits him out. Jonah is a man of swift transition: boat/sea, belly/land. The narrative doesn't linger in the between. For him, for the writers of the Bible, presumably men, for Goodrich and the other male proponents of natural childbirth, transition is not endless and ongoing. It's a finite span of time. Before I gave birth I would have been in this camp, understanding transitions writ large as fleeting by nature: temporary states, bridges between two more solid domains. After birth I know that transitions persist, running below the surface. My body will be preparing for labor long after I leave the hospital; I will be leaving the hospital for months and years after returning home. Part of me will stay in the delivery room vent, no matter what else I am doing or where else I exist.

Once discharged we don't go home—not yet. We are steadfast in our refusal to return despite reasoning vague and flimsy. The shift will be drawn out, elastic. *I'm not sure I can handle the stairs*, I say, since we live on the third floor. *We need to be as close as possible to Jonah in case the hospital calls*, I say, ignoring the fact that our home is only two miles away. Jed tacitly agrees. No one pokes holes in the logic. What I know: when I return, I will walk through the rooms of my former life and will almost recognize them, but not quite. The worst sort of unfamiliar.

Someone books a room for us at a Hilton Garden Inn a few blocks from the hospital on a busy street beside some chain restaurants and a bus stop. The hotel is sterile in a way meant to make its inhabitants forget the imperfections of the outside world. Its refusal to let in emotion is welcome; adherence to a blueprint leaves no room for human messiness. But quickly we degrade the façade. In the empty minifridge I store vials with drops of the liquid I begin to extract from pumping in strict three-hour intervals through the night while sitting under the flicker of the desk's halogen bulb. I litter postpartum contraptions across the carpet—a sitz bath and cold packs that activate when cracked in half like chicken bones and inflatable cushions and plastic squeeze bottles—sterile parting gifts handed over at the containment room doorway. I drip blood on the toilet seat, then smear it into the plastic when I try to wipe it up. There's so much more blood than I'd been prepared for. *Totally normal,* the donut nurse said, back in the containment room. The discharge instructions tell me not to worry unless the clots grow to the size of golf balls or I soak a pad faster than every hour. This seems extreme, but who am I to argue? This was another thing left out of the diaper commercial. The sticky smell burrows into the clean, folded towels on the bathroom shelf. A card on the nightstand tells us to dial 0 if anything falls short of our expectations. Perfection is their priority!

Biblical Jonah found himself propelled through the whale's gullet and into the warmth of its belly, nestled inside the pulsing tissue of a breathing, swimming, bellowing being. While we attempt to transition to the sterile hotel room, to reassemble our lives without the scaffolding of the hospital schedules and protocols, our Jonah waits in the automated equivalent of the whale, inorganic and stiff, tubes and wires and gauze and syringes and medications churned into his veins.

The three days, it turns out, are a lie. They pass, and the blue cap does indeed come off. Doctors begin to rewarm Jonah like he's a microwaveable meal removed from the freezer, plastic wrapping peeled back at the edge. But something is not right. The doctors consult their screens, their files, whisper to each other. Jonah's transition is not going according to plan.

His brain has begun to seize again, the small one says, leaning toward us like he did in the delivery room. *This time we are having some difficulty getting the seizures under control. Sometimes this happens. Cooling can suppress epileptic activity.* The baby: a collection of latent impulses blocked by an artificial whale. But he cannot stay forever in his blue cap. Jonah the prophet can't stay forever in the whale. At some point he has to emerge into the world. This goes against what I know now about transitions and their ongoingness, but I am learning to accept that there are some rules that aren't evenly applied, and for which there will be glaring discrepancies in logic.

The doctor points to a screen beside the bed where signals sent from neurons to scalp electrodes to machine alert him to hidden chaos. We watch as they load Jonah with one medication, and, when the first line fails to block the stampede, another. He doesn't move.

The baby is not a body but a weapon crammed with artillery. He stays completely still, in spite of the seizing, which makes the seizing hard to believe, just as it was hard to believe that the innocent knocks were in fact dangerous seizures.

We can't take a seizing baby off the floor, the doctor explains. *He's too unstable.* If they can't take him off the floor, they can't wheel him into the MRI machine that will pierce the shield of his skull and survey the damage.

My magnesium drip successfully spared me this fate of electricity shooting random, pinging signals in an escalating cascade, sending me into convulsions. But it isn't as simple as one brain seizing while the other remains calm and unprovoked. The I is bound up with the baby, our fates twined. Pregnancy, it turns out, is not a state that resolves with birth. With the cap off, Jonah is slipping from property of hospital to child of parents. His dark brown hair whorls around his scalp, visible in patches between the electrodes. It's thick enough that, in another timeline, if we were home, I could wash it in the baby bathtub I purchased at the store, using the pink plastic pitcher to rinse with lukewarm water. Without the cap we are inching closer to the moment when I can hold him. I can almost imagine what he will feel like in my arms, the heft of him—he's a healthy seven pounds four ounces, they tell me—but not quite. We're inching closer to the moment when a picture of his brain is taken and the extent of the damage is revealed, which means we're inching closer to some glimpse into our collective future. We're being reabsorbed back into each other. The transition is reversing. Jonah is fleeing shore and returning to the belly of the whale.

Seizure refers to both a medical event wherein the brain emits faulty currents and the act of takeover, as in the occupation of a foreign land by a hostile power. An army swoops in and clots the street with swords and armor, tanks and machine guns. The word derives from the old French *saisir:* to take possession of. Brain under the grip of a hostile, outside force. Invaded and/or haunted. It's hard to stay in the realm of the medical, of misfired signals and electrical imbalances. Because the act of possession requires an actor: fairy, dark and unfeeling, more monster than magic, descending. *Seizure* contains echoes of the word Caesarean—a cutting open, a retrieval—and also *caesura*, an interruption, poetic break slicing a phrase into before and after. It helps me to turn the word over in my mouth, to feel its component sounds on my tongue while watching the still, seizing baby. It removes me from Suite 1089B, where the two of us are being reabsorbed back into each other under careful watch of doctors, and allows me to keep a safe distance.

Can multiple bodies share one self? This is the problem of pregnancy, the push and pull of linked but separate systems which sometimes buckle under weight of competing demands. I am discovering it's also the problem of birth. The child is technically outside the mother but still the mother feels that she must encompass the child. The child, too, shares in the confusion. Theory of mind, the understanding that another person has a consciousness distinct from one's own, does not develop in an infant for many months. The baby may see itself in the curl of its mother's mouth, in the tired bags under her eyes. Mother as self and self as mother.

The whale swallows the prophet Jonah who improbably stays whole, alive and well. Three days later, spat onto dry land, he brushes himself off and travels onward. The story doesn't follow the whale, a kind of mother to Jonah, protecting him from the tumultuous sea, who may be mourning Jonah's departure, nursing the hollow space inside.

He's beautiful, Jed says, peering down at the still baby in a glass case, which means: *Look, our baby exists without his crown of blue.* Now, though, this bundle of electrodes and wires shrouds his skull. Slowly, slowly, his body temperature rises to that of a living being. We are exiting that liminal space in between life and death. Are we parents yet? Will someone tell us when we are? We're exiting the between, but we'll always have one foot stuck there.

His head is swollen from the cold, the nurse who exudes warmth and comfort tells us. She speaks gently, but doesn't pander. *It will take time for its natural shape to emerge.* She warns us not to get used to what we see, not to grow attached to this face, which is not the true face of our baby. It's a kindness, for her to start from the assumption that we aren't already attached, that we are only beginning to piece together our connection.

While we wait for the seizing to stop, she makes arrangements for us to hold Jonah. She has decided it's time for us to dip a toe into the sea of parenthood. She knows we're in no position to take this step on our own accord. That we might stand on the shore indefinitely if left to our own devices. First, she argues with the technician who wants to change the position of some of the electrodes on his head. *No,* she says, *not now. You can come back later.* She insists some things can wait.

She pages the respiratory therapist, a wiry bald man with a pulsing forehead vein and maroon scrubs, for assistance with his tubes. Together they rearrange chairs, press buttons on his pumps, untangle cords. Finally, she reaches into the glass box for the baby. *Shh,* she says to him as she lifts, though he is absolutely silent.

I suspend Jonah atop my arms in what might look like a cradle but is too rigid to be an embrace. He needs to be held at exactly the right angle, so my arms must remain flat as a surgical table. The blue ventilator tube, plunged into his mouth and held in place by a toothed plastic clamp, and IV lines speared into his hands and arms, cannot be disturbed. His nose is mercifully spared: a perfect set of tiny nostrils, flattened by gestation and compression and descent, dot both sides of a cartilaginous ridge. Wires measuring his oxygen saturation and heart rate and electrodes charting brain misfirings must remain slack and unkinked, and bags connected to his respirator must remain flat, for the smallest fold could disturb the flow of medication or oxygen in or the flow of toxins and information out, setting off the beeps and alarms that populate the NICU halls, lulling its inhabitants—the whole place a serene emergency.

How did Jonah in the whale track time? Did he tick marks against the walls of the whale's stomach with the edge of a fingernail, counting the rocking of the waves, or did he rely on some internal sense like hunger or thirst that might map minutes passing? Or did Jonah give up time altogether because it stopped mattering in that growling belly under the sea, briny waves lapping at thick blubber like some distant lullaby, his body tossed from side to side inside sticky gut, and only impose the stamp retroactively, for the sake of narrative? Modern religious scholars sidestep the bulky inconvenience of time by arguing, for example, that each day of creation stands for thousands of years. Time watered down to metaphor. This way, they reconcile history and myth, science and belief. This way, they approach something they call truth.

Are my Jonah's days—his three days in the cap—truly days or are they weeks or months or years or something else entirely that the word time and all its associated measurements and contraptions cannot begin to describe—a presence removed from known rhythms, an existence in heaving folds, a hovering—neither life nor death? The order of the events as I remember them may be different from the order in which they occurred, but that does not mean they are less correct. Biblical Jonah in the darkness would know this to be true.

We do not move. The nurse secures Jonah's ventilator tube to my collarbone with a tear of medical tape. It's an action endowed with humanity, the way she smooths the adhesive to my skin, binding me to him. One electrode dislodges from his scalp and clinks against my arm. I'm surprised at how cold it is. *Don't worry about it*, she preempts. *We can reattach it later.* It's an inversion of Harry Harlow's wire mother experiment, testing my capacity for attachment to a wire baby; in the study, the monkeys bonded with the soft artificial mother over the wire one, but here we are betting that I can overcome proven biology to bond with the wire baby.

I hold the body, but not too tight. He emits a viscous smell: glue-clumped hair and blood-caked stump of umbilical cord. The skin of his calf is flaky and dry against my arm which is still swollen from my own syndrome. It's a reminder that he isn't all medical contraption kept alive by the whirring, hissing ventilator, that he's organic and living, whatever that means. He isn't fully wire.

The ventilator heaves a small sigh, continues on with its work. Jonah feels half baby and half machine—an entity I do not know how to nurture yet cannot discard as entirely mechanical bundle.

What if Jonah stayed forever in the whale's belly, afraid of shore, never begging God for release with his promise of obedience? Would a biblical book bear his name? Would we read his story each year on the day Jews atone to their ever-silent god? What if my Jonah stayed in his equivalent of the whale's belly—not the womb but the cooling cap? What if he never took off his blue hat, never went for his MRI? What if he remained frozen here in a state of silent seizing, behind the doors of the Mother/Baby Suite?

I don't think I can do this, I say into the glass box when no one else is looking. I can't hold him again because to hold him too long or too often might confer too much stimulation on his rattled body. I press two fingers gently to his arm, the way the nurse taught. *I don't think it's possible for me to do this*, I tell him again, in case he did not understand me the first time. He moves his lips into an o and as I lean in for his reply his fist begins to knock knock knock against the invisible door—not a response but an electrical takeover of his mind.

After another load of Fosphenytoin—a powerful seizure medication brought in when the phenobarbital alone fails to do its job—dampens Jonah's brain, smashing chaos into a flat line, we go to a Chinese restaurant near the hospital. I walk slowly, holding Jed's arm, and our families wait at the busy corners for me to catch up. Jed carries the plastic bag with my stash of supplies in his other hand: pads and squirt bottles and the donut pillow, which I need in order to sit. We cross the bridge over Michigan Avenue, and I witness the world preserved: cars run yellow lights; mannequins stare from windows; clouds threaten rain. This preservation has taken place in a jar. I can see the contents but the seal is tight and I can't enter.

Inside the Chinese restaurant the owner hovers over our table and tells us about his award-winning Peking duck which must be ordered in advance. *You didn't call ahead,* he scolds. *What a shame. It's ok. You'll come back. You'll order it next time.* He flashes a smile I don't trust.

Our food arrives. People pass dishes of dumplings and chicken and broccoli. Spoonfuls of oil erupt on the white tablecloth. The tea is lukewarm and pale. When we finish and stand to leave, the owner is waiting by the door, thumbing through receipts. He turns to me and says, *Congratulations!*

It catches me off guard. What could anyone possibly be congratulating me for? I walk through the door as quickly as I can hobble.

Did someone tell him about Jonah? I ask, once we are crammed outside under the restaurant's awning. The rain comes now in thick sheets. I can't see across the street. For a moment no one answers. We stare at the rain.

My father-in-law says, finally, *I think he assumed you're still pregnant.*

And I look down and see that my stomach has not returned to its usual size, as though it's still waiting for my son to emerge from under the briny foam of the dark sea.

Wild West

The midwife emerges through the open cabin door below me. On her left cheek is a streak of blood, like war paint. Has she had no time to clean my blood off? She appears to have aged rapidly, her wrinkles set deeper into her face, her whiskers darker than before. My husband stops his pacing.

You have a boy, she announces to my husband, though he already knows, I want to say—she has already announced this fact, of course. Has she forgotten in the tumult?

A boy, a boy, a boy: it's a chant that will follow me wherever I float. I will hear it no matter how far I travel. *A boy, a boy, a boy.* The other side of the coin: *a mother, a mother, a mother.* I am not sure a ghost can be a mother. I will try to find out.

I swing down from the roof and follow my husband inside after the midwife, expecting my feet to catch on the doormat, though of course they don't—I have no feet. Here, home, it is too easy to forget about my new disembodied state, lulled by the deep familiarity of the place. It's too easy to mistakenly apply the rules of the living to myself.

An unfamiliar shade of curtain hangs in the lone window, an ugly periwinkle with bunches of small white flowers. A bar of pink soap molded into a neat oval, fancier than the rough beige kind I buy from the general store, sits on the sill. Beside the fire hangs a rabbit, tawny-brown and ready to be skinned. Did my husband trap it? How has he had the time?

He walks toward our bed, bending down to avoid a low beam. It's a beautiful bed, a maple four-poster we brought with us, in pieces, from back east. It is the nicest item we own, the only real piece of furniture. It took up too much space in the wagon but I insisted. *It's not practical,* he said, but he wanted it, too.

A foot sticks out from under the quilt. Whose foot is that? Am I somehow in two places at once? Have I reentered my body? My husband tiptoes closer. He takes off his hat and holds it between his calloused hands. The floorboards creak no matter how careful his steps, the way they always have.

Busy morning we've had here, the midwife whispers. She holds a finger up to her lips. In her other arm lies a bundle wrapped in the blue blanket I knit and left behind before I went to the outhouse and then the preacher's house and the shed and the coffin and the hills. Could this be my baby? Has he somehow survived, a miracle?

Let the poor girl rest. Doc administered a dram of chloroform to help at the end, with the long pains, she explains. She pulls down the edge of my quilt to show a sleeping face, fat pink cheeks framed in blond curls, a bit of soft pink shoulder from the top of a lace-fringed dressing gown. I do not recognize her.

My husband leans down to kiss the glistening forehead of this stranger. The midwife shuffles her stockinged feet across the dirt floor. I am pressed flat against the ceiling, more of the house than of the people who inhabit it. Since I left the comfort of our cabin for the outhouse, my husband has managed to mourn me and our child and he has married another woman and she has carried and birthed his child anew. This second wife lies in her birthing bed, which was once my bed, recovering from the ordeal. It comes at me all at once, the way tornados swept across the open fields on our journey west. Time has compressed and fanned back out. No time has passed and also much.

The woman, this second wife, winces under my husband's touch. Her eyes flutter but don't open. She's alive.

The midwife takes the baby and places him in the cradle, unwraps the blanket and dips a finger in an open tub of salve, which she smears across the stub of black cord tied off with white string. I float up so I can look down at the baby's face. It's thin and pale with two deep-set blue eyes and a shock of dark hair. The darkness of the hair confronts the brightness of the eyes, as though they belong to two different beings and have been melded together through strange alchemy. It opens its lips and lets out a small squeal, more animal than human.

The second wife wakes. She props herself up and sips a gelatinous broth the midwife spoons into her mouth. She clenches, probably to stifle the pain that lingers. I can tell she doesn't want anyone to know she suffers, but I know.

I look back at the sleeping bundle of baby in its cradle, the cradle that once waited empty for my child, and I recognize something in its face. I look closer: my son bubbles within this baby, a dybbuk. I know it at once, a truth, the way an infant knows how to drink milk at birth, the way its arms splay out to protect itself from a fall—instinct sure and solid.

My mother told me of this phenomenon, the dybbuk, an evil spirit inhabiting the body of a living being, as part of her death-bed confession. She worried one might overtake her as the spirit left her body. That her body would die a slow death, emptying out bit by bit, and in the space a spirit might nestle inside before she left completely. She said she had always feared being possessed by one as the price she'd have to pay for hiding that she was a Jewess; a divine punishment for turning her back on her people. She spoke of stories she'd heard passed down through her mother's line: beautiful, virginal women possessed on the eve of their nuptials, babbling incoherently as the rabbi tried to chase the invading spirit out of them; and of young, fresh mothers suddenly taken to bed, bodies overtaken with an evil temptation like the wily snake from the garden, soon rendered unable to speak.

The Bible, my mother said, was filled with such examples of dybbuks if you looked closely enough. Jonah, for instance, a prophet possessed when he refused to obey God and travel to Ninevah. I knew the Bible from church and told her there was no mention of a dybbuk, not anywhere as far as I could tell, not even in the stranger books full of fire and brimstone—only Satan, who was something different—but this did not dissuade her. Her mind was already half outside her body by that point; she could not be reasoned with. I told her that this fear of the dybbuk was only a superstition, a silly thought embedded in her rattled mind as it neared its end. *No such thing,* I told her. She shook her head wildly with what little strength she had left.

But when she died, I could not rid myself of the image she left behind—dybbuk as a person slivered down the middle, half of this world and half of another. The skin a sheath disguising the duality underneath.

The dybbuk here in the cradle is not the terrifying creature my mother feared; he is an innocent, untimely cleaved from his original body, a soul alone and desperate and in search of shelter. My child: abandoned in the gray space between life and death, afforded no beginning or end, granted no burial and recipient of no mourning. He took no first breath and so can find no rest in death. He needs a home for his spirit and has found one here, in this other creature. I kneel down beside him. My knees don't touch the ground. I have no knees, I remember.

A boy, a boy, a boy.

I will find you, I promised him, and I have.

Chicago

The morning of the fourth day, and Jonah, blocks away in his glass bed, remains an enigma, a hovering question mark. The darkness curling through his brain has not been examined and interpreted. The doctors say it's there, only we can't see it. If we can't see it, maybe it doesn't exist. There are two babies: the exterior one, perfectly normal if you ignore the breathing tube, and the scarred interior they claim lies under the surface. When I try to envision his brain I generate various competing pictures: a postapocalyptic cratered landscape of rocks and dust; sparking electrical wires; a black hole of nothingness. I can't make sense of the colliding imagery which only adds to the sense of chaos.

Nothing about him will change once we know, Jed says, about the extent of the injury. He wants to comfort me, but it's frustrating, the way he can stay philosophical at a moment like this. He means that what's there is already there, which yes, of course, but also that rationale makes no difference to me. I sit at the desk across from the hotel-room bathroom, moving the notepad and lamp out of the way to make space for the hospital-grade pump I've rented on the postpartum nurse's advice. I've only recently moved out of the realm of rusty pipe and, like a flat Candy Land figure, into the land of colostrum, which the nurses call liquid gold. I dutifully extract the droplets, which are more dirty yellow than gold and hardly seem capable of providing basic nutrition, much less the magical healing promised in their nickname. Still, I pump, because it gives me something to do, a way to be of use for the baby who may or may not be mine.

He'll still be our Jonah, no matter what the MRI shows, Jed continues. He sits up in bed, a look of deep resolve on his face. He means what he says. He takes his role as father seriously. He is able to apply his strict ethical principles no matter the circumstances of his emotions, the consummate principled lawyer. But I rely on intuitive impulses, leaving me less ready to commit.

We've named Jonah, which is a step towards claiming him as our baby, but I'm still waiting for the doctors to tell me who he is based on what the MRI shows. I want some sort of conclusion to our story, however untidy. I am striving for a finish line that keeps disappearing over the horizon and out of reach as we approach. I watch Jed, try to emulate his certainty, but I can't make myself fall in line.

Downstairs I realize I've forgotten the colostrum in the minifridge. Back in the elevator bank off the lobby, a woman pushes a stroller back and forth. We wait and I press the button again because still the elevator hasn't arrived. It's critical that it come. I assume a baby lies inside but can't look—the stroller is a forcefield repelling my glance. The intensity is so strong that once we finally escape it via elevator my eyes flush with what must be tears, expelled by the great release of tension.

When we arrive at the NICU the medical team is already bustling around the room, preparing to take Jonah to the MRI, that mystical place deep in the blinding-white center of the hospital where fates are decided. We cannot accompany him. The rabbi from my parents' synagogue has flown in for the day to lend support. He joins us in the Mother/Baby suite while we say our goodbyes and, as nurses begin to wheel Jonah away, asks: *Do you want to say a prayer?* He is sensitive to the fact that this is not a foregone conclusion, the desire for prayer, that our religion does not require belief in the efficacy of supplication, or belief in God at all. I don't believe in God, but I do. I don't have a baby, but I do. I don't believe the words will matter, but I do. Or at least I say them, repeat short Hebrew phrases of the *Mi Shebeirach,* the prayer for healing, after the rabbi, phrases that are all sound and no sense—not to me, at least. I repeat the words. Jed does, too, looking grateful to be given a map, some sort of ritual to guide him through this moment, though for him religion has even less bearing; his Jewish identity is purely cultural, the question of a divine force utterly laughable. He's the grandchild of a man who'd cast aside the Yiddishkeit of his immigrant parents—the old traditions and superstitions—and proudly remade himself as a suave and worldly Kansas City lawyer and contemporary-art collector, replacing the ancient with the modern. Jed inherited this outlook.

As we finish the prayer, a collection of hospital personnel in matching green scrubs wheels Jonah out of the room, and, at that moment, what I really want is a donut to offer his nurse, one final plea, as she rounds the corner and disappears out of sight.

Erik Erikson's reimagining of development envisioned childhood, beginning at birth, as a series of crises to be resolved before forging ahead into the abyss of adulthood. Adulthood too was marked by similar struggles. Each stage he presented like a marquee: Trust v. Mistrust, Autonomy v. Shame and Doubt, Initiative v. Guilt. Until now I had marched forward through the stages of life more or less as expected: graduating from high school, then college, finding and navigating my first jobs, getting engaged, then married, and finally pregnant. I wasn't on autopilot, I thought my actions through, but I was more or less able to follow a well-trod path.

Now, though, I don't see any markers pointing the way. The walls are white and decorated with interchangeable landscapes like the halls of the hospital. Erikson has no phase that neatly corresponds to "waiting for first child to complete MRI scan of brain." The other models of parenthood I see around me, like the mother with the baby in the elevator bank, are no help, either. They represent a parenthood so distant from what I'm experiencing it would be unrecognizable–that is, if I could bring myself to look.

Before: I imagined myself living that now-alien version of parenthood, wheeling my baby, tucked in a stroller, to the same coffee shop where I eavesdropped on the doula. I'd sit on the patio while the baby slept. I'd sip iced green tea under a tree and read a book and talk to a friend or stare at the sun's waffling pattern on the pavement. The baby would wake and cry and I'd nurse it back to sleep. I would be deeply rooted in the Generativity v. Stagnation phase of my development, the one Erikson reserved for the reproductive years, with laid-back, early-motherhood time on my hands—sleep deprived, sure, but giddy and vacant of the sort of worries (of schools and bullies and peer pressure and depression and drinking) that would, I knew, come with time. The kinds that evolve as a baby becomes a child becomes a person–as they, too, progress through their own timeline. But those worries wouldn't set in right away. For the moment I would live in the unburdened present, even if that present was only part of the whole.

Now: I'm not allowed to go into the bowels of the hospital with my son, can only watch his cart disappear into whiteness. The door shuts between us. STAFF ONLY. But that I can't follow doesn't matter. I feel the white walls of the hallway he descends close in, fluorescent light quivering down, one day and the next day and the day after and for many more days stretched out in a line so long I can't see its end. I will feel them around me when I pull a shirt over my head and when I pee and when I see a pothole in the road ahead while driving from hotel to hospital and when I drink at the water fountain in the NICU hallway and a rivulet curves down my chin and, later, when I rinse shampoo from matted hair and write an email and laugh at a stupid joke. This is the beginning of the rest of our lives. Each day will be a version of watching him get wheeled away for an MRI. Little by little it will grow less terrifying, but the claustrophobia will never disappear completely.

Except, returning to Erikson, he didn't actually believe in that arbitrary line where we jump from the curb into traffic, from childhood into adulthood. The lines between his stages were not so thick. That had been my own misunderstanding about the way life would unfold. Erikson understood that crises continue and continue, complicating a person's trajectory. Stakes mount as child, then adolescent, parent then grandparent, advance through requisite stages—a video game where the player slays the first monster only to move on to face another: more savage, more cruel, and now with nine lives to boot. He would have intuited how the film of MRI day will coat the rest of my life.

While Jonah slips deep into the MRI's clanking tube the staff convinces us to eat lunch in the hospital cafeteria. They assure us we have time to kill before the results come through. Time has become a monster—Grendel, or one of the shape-shifting video game antagonists—a minotaur to slaughter if we can make our way through the labyrinth. It's morphed into something unlike the version of time I knew before Jonah. The three days turned four have invaded every crevice with their blinking countdown, but a day has also become a meaningless mode of measurement. The minutes are interminable and lightning-fast at the same time and the result is that I have no sense of time passing.

Don't wait around all day, the staff says, *you'll go crazy.* What they fail to understand: we have already descended into quicksand, feet sinking further with each movement, no matter how slight.

Nothing's going to change while you're gone, they assure us when we hesitate. Meaning the damage was there and will still be there when we return, which was Jed's too-logical argument from before. Meaning Jonah's brain will heal or shatter, or whatever it is going to do or has already done, regardless of when we hear the description of the image those magnets retrieve. Meaning we can stay or go, pray or not pray, cry or not cry, pace or not pace, think or not think. Nothing we do can change a thing. It's all written out, dark indelible ink—has been since he emerged from the black box of my womb, entered the blue cap of the Mother/Baby Suite. That sort of fatalism is a tough pill to swallow, more of a piece with Calvinism than my freewheeling Judaism.

After school some days I would go to my grandmother's house and play *MawMaw May I* with her on the front porch of her house. She'd sip iced water from a reused red Solo cup (child of the Depression), its white edge stained with red lipstick, and try to make her instructions so complex I'd forget the magic phrase and return to start.

Sometimes the streetcar rumbled past and we'd interrupt the game to wave at passengers: strange conglomeration of fanny-packed tourists snapping photos and weary commuters waiting for the hot sun to set.

Per Erikson, I was likely in the stage of Industry v. Inferiority, a relatively stable time of identity solidification in childhood, before the tumult of adolescence. I see myself there now, against the white stucco exterior, skipping and jumping in a straight line according to my grandmother's instructions, trying to follow the rules, to make it to the end, to get to the next stage. I worked under the assumption that if I did those things, if I tried hard enough, if I applied myself, I would get where I wanted to go. I had so little sense of the way the world could change in an instant, how external forces tear in and uproot. Perhaps that's the crux of Erikson's theory—that childhood writ large is all about solidifying a sense of stable selfhood and control, only to get to adulthood and have it all crumble with the dawning realization that control is an illusion because death and decay lurk, and maybe the stability of self is a delusion, too.

For a moment, in the bustle of the cafeteria, regarding the menus posted above the grill station and salad bar, I forget this is the day our fate (we, by now, entangled with Jonah) will be decided, and so I choose a burrito, stand in line for the cashier, gather silverware and napkins, find our table. I am lulled by the hum of plates clattering, phones vibrating against tables, cash register drawers clicking open and closed. Then I see a huddle of green scrubs, remember where we are and what we are waiting for, and stare down at my overstuffed tortilla, blackened chicken, and lumps of rice and beans erupting from its gashes.

I find the table with our families and the rabbi and sit and take a bite of burrito because it seems rude not to and, somehow, I have not stopped caring about decorum, about what I'm supposed to do and what's expected of me, not completely. Jed forks up his salad, neatly sprayed with slivers of vegetables—the smarter choice, the one more befitting the occasion. I cut my burrito and move the pieces around so it looks partially eaten—maybe one-third or one-half gone—all presentation on the plate, all optical illusion.

After we deposit our trash and return our trays, we ride the elevator back to the floor and a nurse leads us to Jonah. He has returned from the hospital's bowels, and no longer has his own private suite labeled with glaring euphemism. Now they've placed him in the general population of the NICU, albeit in the wing for those requiring tubes to breathe for them. There's yet another section, on the other side, for the healthier babies who can breathe on their own. There are so many hidden levels in this hospital that aren't revealed until you descend or ascend to them. Perhaps there are hidden levels within Erikson, too—sublevels between the main ones, only visible if you manage to get to them.

I sit in the cushioned recliner and Jed pulls a plastic chair beside me. The space allotted to us is small and we can hear parents and nurses chatter on the other side of the sliding door. It's hard to imagine being capable of that sort of small talk again. Jonah lies completely still. I almost want him to seize again to remind me he's here.

Jed gets up to wash the milk-crusted pump equipment at the hall sink so it's ready to use when the alarm goes off. I'm in stasis, waiting for the MRI results. Sometimes I realize I've been holding my breath and remind myself to exhale. At least the schedule of pumping and pain meds gives me something to do with my body, some task to focus my mind on, a miniature sort of Eriksonian mission to complete so I can proceed towards the next level. Jed shuts the sliding door quietly behind him as though afraid to wake Jonah, pretending he is really sleeping instead of felled by barbiturates. We could drop a brick on the hard floor and he wouldn't flinch; the make-believe is a comfort to us both.

I stay behind, beside Jonah. The whole time we wait for the doctor, I sit beside him. In his book, *Childhood and Society,* Erikson describes the situation of the womb as one of *chemical exchange.* Mother releases molecules, baby absorbs. The next situation gets ushered in when the two bodies disconnect. He doesn't account for cases of a faulty link between mother and baby, where the severing happens undetected, before its time. Maybe, in those situations, the mother tries to recreate the situation in a vain attempt to fix the unfixable.

Jonah's eyes remain tightly sealed, lids sprawling with purple veins. Legs womb-bent, arms phenobarbital-flopped. Head bare but for stubborn pocks of glue. A heaviness surrounds him, his course now determined, imprinted—an image. We wait to hear what it is. I sit beside him and watch his chest rise and fall as the tube connected to the ventilator conveys breath, and somewhere, on another floor or perhaps in another building, a person in a white coat peers at a screen. She straightens her glasses, pulls up her stool, magnifies each lobe and cross-section, leans in closer, determines what remains.

Wild West

The midwife packs up her things in her satchel and says she'll return tomorrow. On her way out, she gives the cradle a rock where the second baby and my dybbuk child lie. The baby inside is not one or the other but both.

I stay in the ceiling and watch as the second wife changes her soiled dressings. She places the old ones in a tin can for the washing. Her face bears a look of disgust when she sees what's come out of her body.

Later my husband and the second wife wait for the baby they do not realize is also mine to wake and cry out and feed and sleep. The second wife, from time to time, glances in my direction and flinches. Does she see me, or evidence of me, moving through the air? She turns back to check—was her vision real?—but I have moved behind a chest of drawers on the other side of the room. It takes no time to disappear from one place and reappear in another. We, ghost and human mother, are linked through this baby of ours, connected through the molecules of air that hang, still and smoky from the fire in the hearth, in the cabin.

The waiting and the waking and the crying and the feeding continue on and on, in a loop.

When no one is paying attention, I like to swoop down to the baby until I can almost feel its breath against my cheek—if I could feel, and if I had a cheek, I would feel it.

When the baby sleeps in its cradle the second wife pulls back the blankets to examine it and make sure it's still breathing, to make sure it's still hers. Sometimes she wakes him from fragile sleep with her checking and rechecking. I can tell she knows something isn't right but she hasn't figured out what it is.

Chicago

Late afternoon, the neonatologist leads us into a windowless room with a plastic-covered couch and three plastic-covered armchairs, and reads aloud from the MRI report she holds in her lap. This is not the same, small doctor who spoke to us in the delivery room, when we stood in a field, weeds wrapping around us. Dr R's not working today. It seems unfair that the doctors can leave the pull of Jonah, splayed in his glass bassinet, take off their scrubs, retreat, wave-like, while we are tethered to him. This new doctor pauses for us to take in each line of the dense medical language I don't understand. Black spots spin across my eyes; I have forgotten to breathe.

For four days, the doctors have tried to cushion the blow, repeating over and over again that the MRI, while the most predictive diagnostic for this kind of injury, is far from perfect. They have warned us that two babies with identical MRI results might have two drastically divergent outcomes. The story the image conveys will contain only the barest outlines of a prognosis, they explained. Despite the caveats, I wanted to know. I wanted a solid thing to hold onto—any fact—or so I thought. Now I'm less sure. Perhaps it would have been better to stay in the between, but it's too late.

The doctor begins to describe lobes and peaks and extensions, deep structures and cortical regions and subdural hemorrhage. She conjures an entire topography, but we don't see the image. We only get words that describe this picture which itself is extracted via magnet. Abstraction from abstraction from abstraction. We are floating so far from firmament.

What does it mean? Jed asks the doctor, after her recitation is over. His voice comes from a distance.

My legs have melded with the plastic. I cannot tell where I end and the couch begins. Part of me was convinced, until this point, no matter the odds, that the unscathed head under the blue cap held an unscathed brain. That, like I'd posited to Dr. G. back in the delivery room, the doctors were wrong. He couldn't have been injured or I'd have known. I had birthed him, after all. But they were not wrong. I, too, have questions, but I can't figure out how to ask them. What do you call the condition where your tongue can't find its own words? Does this signal a progression from which there's no hope of recovery? Will I ever think a new thought again? Can the mind rebound from this fate?

You'll have to wait for the neurologist to explain it more tomorrow, the doctor says, refusing to translate further than she already has. *He's in clinic today uptown and I don't feel comfortable interpreting the results. This isn't my area of expertise.* She pauses and her inhale echoes in the small room. *But, of course, it would be better if this damage were not there.*

Is this what you expected to see? I manage. Now that I can't hold onto the hope that the doctors were simply wrong, that there was no injury, the meeting or exceeding or falling short of arbitrary expectation seems a reasonable recalibration. I am trying to locate myself with any clues available—lost spelunker deep in a cave, headlamp batteries long dead, feeling walls for grooves and curves as though they might provide a map.

To be honest, she says, folding the edge of the paper, *based on his clinical presentation, I expected worse.*

I feel bits of my cafeteria burrito crystalizing inside.

I'm not sure what all the doctor's words mean. I don't know exactly what terms like "deep nuclei" or "mass effect" refer to. I'm partially relieved by her reticence to decode. Some things are better left untranslated. Jewish prayers, for example, sound vastly more tolerable in Hebrew where they remain mysterious and mellifluous, even poetic. In translation, they morph into the weird and superstitious, scattered with terrifying beasts and mythical, fiery rocks and all-knowing beings bent on destruction. All of us under the thumb of a vengeful, petty, selfish god. I've learned enough in the last few days to understand that the valence of the words I don't understand is negative, that it would be better if they were replaced with other words. I know the report describes a pathological occurrence, a pattern of brain matter that should not be. I may not speak the language of the hospital, but I don't need it all spelled out. This way I can still hide behind the things I don't know. It's an embrace of ignorance, a temporary reprieve.

Medical language, like parts of the bible, can be impenetrable to the lay person, waiting to be deciphered by the elite few who hold specialized knowledge. Biblical exegesis is the fancy term for the way scholars interpret the text's often cryptic stories and laws. It's a kind of translation, but concerned with uncovering deep meaning, meaning elided by the swift transitions of the text, the bare-bones writing, rather than mere surface-level decoding. Jewish practice is based more on this interpretation—the rabbinic laws of the Mishna and Gemara spun out from the Bible over millennia in exile—than it is on the actual words in the original books.

The MRI is also not a standalone text. It doesn't exist in a vacuum, but in tandem with a clinical picture, the doctors keep reminding us. The problem is that Jonah is incapacitated by the drugs, and, even if he were awake, he's only four days old. There's not much a four-day-old baby can indicate about his mental capacities. There's very little context he can provide. We don't have a Talmud to illuminate him. *We'll have to wait and see*, the neonatologist told us. But what she really meant was that Jed and I would have to wait and see. Jonah won't stay here forever under the NICU's care; new babies will cycle through and she will forget about us, about him.

That night Jed and I escape the NICU and order room service so we don't have to talk to anyone else. Meals still mark what's left of time, punctuate our waiting, though I no longer desire food and now I'm not sure what I'm waiting for. We're freed from the countdown but we're still tied to waiting, only this time there's no finish line.

I don't feel sick; I simply have no hunger. Hunger feels impossibly far away. *I'll skip dinner*, I say to Jed. But he insists I eat. Since we've left the hospital and the supervision of postpartum nurses, he has taken up the reins of my care, watching me for signs of deterioration on multiple fronts, but he seems to have been drugged by the doctor's report, staring past me as he speaks, his words slow and deliberate like it's taking him every effort to form them. He'd cried in the family meeting room after the doctor left to let us absorb the information. Big, heaving, choking sobs that terrified me because they confirmed that, yes, things were as bad as they seemed and also comforted me because, no, I was not alone in my despair. Now it seems like that process has emptied him of everything except for the barest outlines of himself.

I scan the menu for the blandest item. *I'll have a baked potato*, I tell him. I learned my lesson with the hospital cafeteria burrito.

You should get more, he says, pointing to the menu. *A potato isn't enough.* I shake my head. He relents, a small shrug. Speaking takes too much energy. His eyes close for a moment as though gathering strength. It doesn't take much to push past him. And at least I have agreed to something.

We sit on the stiff hotel couch until the food arrives. Jed clicks on the TV. It's quiet except for the dings of the game show. We don't talk. I've finally stopped crying, too. I've long bought into the idea of tears as mechanism for releasing emotion, salt and liquid dissolving pain, transforming the feeling into something physical that can then be wiped away. But now I can't see my way to an exit. Pain is everywhere and everything: dark paneled walls, sealed-shut windows, sun setting between towering buildings, game show flashing, mute, in front of us. There's no point.

Someone knocks, sets the food down on the coffee table, leaves. Probably the staff are trained to ignore the strange things they might see in these rooms, for example two nearly comatose people, red-eyed and sitting vacantly in front of "Wheel of Fortune."

We examine our tray. Under the dish cover there's no butter for my potato and the restaurant has already closed, so I eat half of it plain—mealy, soapy, rough. I would complain to the front desk about this, follow their directions to dial 0 to report any substandard experiences, request my money back, but I worry the slightest discontentment expressed will demand karmic repayment; the nurse might return the donut uneaten. Besides, I don't really taste anything anyway, and butter wouldn't change that.

When the alarm wakes me to pump in the night, Jed is sitting up in bed reading on his phone. It's dark except for the yellow glow of his screen and the red numbers of the alarm clock.

What are you looking at? I ask.

Something about HIE.

What's that?

What Jonah has. Or maybe what happened to him. He puts down the phone. *I don't know which.*

Somehow, despite hovering by Jonah's side, listening to lists rattled during rounds day after day, sitting in the room with the doctor who read the MRI results, I've missed the actual diagnosis. It has yet to occur to me that there exists an official name for almost suffocating your child before birth. It seemed so awful and so unheard of that I didn't think to ask if there was a word for it. This label gives the amorphous thing meaning, shape.

Hypoxic Ischemic Encephalopathy: the technical way of saying that the vessels binding me to Jonah did not deliver enough blood, or that, somehow, my body drained the blood of oxygen. The condition used to be called birth asphyxia. I suspect someone changed the wording to quell panic, or at least delay it so the overflow occurs far from the doctor announcing the sentence. Changing the name was an exercise in medical translation, demonstrating the significance of choosing words not only for plain sense but for implication and association, for sound and feeling. When a translator translates a poem it's the same thing; they consider assonance and rhyme and the number of syllables and if all of that facilitates communication of the intended meaning.

HIE makes no assumptions regarding the mechanism for clamping, nor its effects. It's not a diagnosis in the sense of cancer or lupus or hemophilia. HIE describes the event, fleeting, that imprints on the body—the equivalent of a car crash crushing the femur or a shallow-water dive severing the spine. It names the moment in time when a brain drains of blood and emerges white with emptiness; it names the act of eviction, though no one can pinpoint exactly when this occurred in the black box of my womb, and no one can explain why. Everything is conjecture.

Midrashim are explanatory stories written to fill in the myriad blank spaces of the Torah, the conceptions and births and deaths that take place in single sentences. Jonah's HIE midrash might be cord compression, or some change in my blood pressure that impacted flow through the placenta. There are a million midrashim I could devise to try to understand what has happened to us, and all of them, like Schrödinger's cat, will be equally true and untrue.

In the original Hebrew, Jonah is not stuck in the belly of the whale, per se, but in the belly of a *dag gadol*—a big fish—unspecified species, but fish, not mammal. Fish as in offspring born via eggs hatched, not kindled inside the belly of a mother. A big fish has none of the roundness of a whale, none of the strength of its tail emerging out of surf, spout spewing waves of its own making back to sea. A fish feels no sadness or compassion, does not nurture the way a whale does (in our imaginations, at least), with heaves and songs and nudging gestures towards its young. A fish has aggregated no mythology. Creature unlike the storied, majestic whale—some symbolic god, sought after, prized, mystical. Perhaps this is why we've replaced fish with whale in some translations, and also in the popular consciousness. A whale might have mercy on poor Jonah as it spits him out to safety on dry land. A fish is all bony skeleton and tiny, empty eyes surrounded by flecked scales, barnacles. Not evil but neutral, amoral, cold-blooded.

Like the whale that was actually a fish, the blue cap was actually white. I don't discover this until months later, when I finally look at the first pictures we took of Jonah, so different from the ones I'd imagined taking when, post-epidural, I asked my friend to bring our camera. It's then that I notice a white sheath over the blue, blue only peeking out from the sides and on the strap, pulled tight under his chin. In the intervening time, the blue cap had become my short-hand for the days when Jonah was born but not fully alive, when he hovered in his frozen, seizing limbo. The vividness of the color in my mind, a saturated royal blue, allowed me to hold onto these days, to try to make sense of them as a container of my proto-mother-hood. White would have been too meek, too easy to overlook. White could not encapsulate the way the four days held me and him in a stretched-out timeline all our own. Blue, like the biblical whale, has more staying power, more gravitas. I've mistranslated my memories. In the photos, Jonah is strung with more tubing than I remember. More equipment than baby. More white than blue. More fish than whale. Whale is just the story I've been telling myself.

You look like you're waiting for the executioner, the tropical Santa of a neurologist jokes when he comes into the family meeting room, where yesterday the doctor told us it would be better if brain damage had not occurred. The hospital has a method for cordoning off par-ents like us so we don't infect the rest of the place with our despair: the containment room on the postpartum floor, the Mother/Baby Suite, the family meeting room. These innocuously named locales where we can mourn for a baby who is still alive without scaring the others.

Together we trek down the hall to the glass crib. We're waiting for the neurologist to interpret the results for us. He explains that he needs to ground them in the context of a clinical exam. He taps on the soles of each of Jonah's feet, lifts his rag-doll arms. Jonah's eyes remain sealed shut. His hair, once covered in the blue cap, is now slicked back with baby oil the nurses used to try to unstick the electrode glue. He doesn't move because he is no longer seizing, which means he looks less alive than before. He is still a baby of this hospital, its sterile air pushed to inflate his lungs via long, blue tube.

He's snowed, the neurologist says, *so I can't examine much yet. We have to wait for him to come out from under it all before I can tell you more.*

I see our baby emerging from the avalanche, shrugging sheets of ice off his shoulders, shaking water from his hair, looking around the frozen landscape, crawling into the distance.

Can you meet a person when they are unconscious? I want to ask the neurologist. *Have I met my baby? If I haven't, is he mine?*

No doctor anticipates such questions. They don't expect to be tasked with making meaning out of the set of facts written in their electronic medical records. They cloak pronouncements in the anatomical, in technical phrases like burst suppression and fetal acidosis. I would ask for definitions, for translations, but I don't want those words, static and arcane, to come to life in front of me.

Before I learned the medical terminology, before our experience was given the contours of a name—HIE—what happened to Jonah was as simple as the plunging of brain into vacuum, a free-fall so complete and irreversible it defied nature and logic and language. The world before God separated day and night, creating what we call time. Genesis calls this era of pre-time *tohu vavohu,* which translates as "void and without form." The word *tohu* means "emptiness" but *vohu* has no clear meaning. Perhaps it was invented by an ancient scribe to stand alongside *tohu* because rhyme brought cloak of meaning to the abstraction. Together it's a miraculous term, simple and perfect, describing the indescribable, something literally outside the realm of human experience, in a way that makes perfect sense.

Jonah's situation was *tohu vavohu,* and so was mine. The last three days turned to four have taken place outside the realm of human experience, in a place of empty meaninglessness. We were spinning in the blackness of the proto-universe. In many ways, *tohu vavohu* feels more accurate than HIE. There's nothing neat or logical about where we are, about what happened. It's all chaos.

The neurologist uses his pinkie to illustrate a possible extension of the injury from the cortex into the thalamus, a structure deeper towards the center of the brain, which, for reasons I don't understand, would make Jonah's prognosis significantly worse. The brain, the doctor explains, is made of layers, and the further down into the layers an injury tunnels the more devastating the injury. I have no idea what a thalamus does. He doesn't offer a definition. *Could be a shadow,* he counters, explaining that the image is unclear and might be read variously by different doctors.

The infant brain is remarkably plastic, the neurologist says. He wants to reassure us. Maybe he's uncomfortable with the way I'm lying flat with grief on the plastic sofa. *It can rewire around the injury.* My face sticks to the vinyl, burrowing deeper and deeper, trying to feel its way to the texture of my child's brain.

If you're going to have a brain injury, this is the time to get it, he continues, almost jolly. *Now we just wait and see what Jonah does.* He holds the MRI results in one hand, resting on the shelf of his stomach, atop an almost-neon leaf.

I'll stay home as long as I need to, I say one night in the hotel, maybe the night before or the night after the MRI, maybe the night before or the night after Jed reads me the name and definition of the thing that had overtaken our son. I cannot keep track of the timeline, a tangled mass—owl pellet of fur and teeth and bones unhinged from skeleton and mashed together. The three turned to four days cobbled things together but once that framework evaporates there is no scaffolding.

I am in the middle of my MFA, had planned to take a semester off before returning to finish my degree. *There's no good time to have a baby,* I'd heard over and over again. *You just make it work.* I bought into this line of thinking. I'd not entertained the thought that I'd be in the fraction of a percentage point where things go wildly awry. I would endure the sleepless weeks and return to my life where it had left off, more or less—bound by a baby's schedule, its whims and needs, but otherwise intact. Now seemed as good a moment as any. Besides, maybe the experience of becoming a mother would enrich my writing, expand my horizons, the way so many had promised.

This is more important. I mean Jonah but cannot bring myself to pronounce his name. Not right now.

Shh, Jed says, reaching towards me. He's still tired, emptied out. *We'll figure it out. Don't jump to conclusions.* He tries to run a hand through my hair but it's too tangled from so many days without brushing.

But I'm not jumping to conclusions. I'm trying to preempt fate. My future shuts down each day when I wake and see the objects of the hotel room sharpen into focus, which means I am resuming consciousness in a world where things have gone off-track, where the baby I carried for nine months lies not fully alive many blocks away. I have slipped into a world resembles the one I inhabited before, but the colors clash and the angles are slightly off and I don't know how to move through it without stumbling. I may never write again. Am I still alive?

Jed doesn't notice, but I say *I will give up everything* with a hint of resentment—towards him and the baby, the hospital and doctors, the ventilator and various medications keeping the baby alive, all of it. I have been tricked into thinking I would get one thing and got another instead. The baby in the blue cap is not what I was promised. Immediately I feel regret—that I dared have a baby and also that, after, I dare worry about my own desires when the baby needs me; I feel shame that I have not sufficiently transformed into mother, that I want my old life back.

The biblical story of Abraham's near-killing of his beloved son is known in Hebrew as the *Akedah*, or in English, *The Binding*. Binding as in tightening, as in impeding flow, as in what my body did to the blood on its way to Jonah when he was still in the black box.

In the *Akedah,* a story of parental sacrifice turned inside out, Isaac, led to the top of the mountain, asks his father where the lamb is for the promised sacrifice. Abraham tells him, *God will provide one for the burnt offering my son.* Scholars pore over this phrasing. There is no punctuation in the Torah except for blank spaces used to separate passages. So, is "my son" meant to be set off with a comma? Does "my son" modify the burnt offering? Or is Abraham simply addressing the boy? Jonah's prognosis is full of such blank spaces. Is the darkness on Jonah's MRI an extension into the thalamus or a shadow? How big, exactly, are the "large areas of cortical and subcortical ischemic injury" the radiologist noted, and how little, exactly, are the "scattered small amounts of subdural hemorrhage?" What does "portion" mean when referring to the brain's parietal lobe? Within missing signposts—biblical and medical—lie meaning.

While I toss and turn in the hotel room across town, the baby who is not quite mine remains, per the Hawaiian-shirted neurologist, snowed. His chest rises and falls with the too-perfect mechanical pulse of the ventilator. The nurses give me more of the heart-shaped pieces of fabric to wear in my shirt and then leave by the baby's face so he can smell me and my milk. *He'll get comfort from feeling you close by,* they say. But I'm here and not there, and he is too drugged to have the slight awareness of a newborn, the foggy, blurry perception of the world William James so famously described.

The Akedah is the Torah portion read each year on Yom Kippur, the Jewish Day of Atonement, followed immediately by The Book of Jonah. On this day, the holiest on the calendar, modern rabbis dress in stark white robes and lie prostrate on the ground at certain points in the service, turning the ritual into an elaborate cosplay. They are imitating the temple priests entering the holy of holies deep in the center of the structure. It's designed like the brain: the most critical components buried deepest.

Yom Kippur liturgy includes a prayer, Unetaneh Tokef, about God's impending judgment, particularly brutal to the modern ear and made famous by Leonard Cohen: *Who shall live and who shall die, who in good time, and who by untimely death, who by water and who by fire, who by sword and who by wild beast, who by famine and who by thirst, who by earthquake and who by plague, who by strangulation and who by lapidation.* When I read the translated column in the siddur, sitting beside my parents after the kid's service had finished, I was half-shocked at the violent god no one around me discussed, but half-overjoyed. Finally, here was my version of God, powerful and involved, not distant or remote. A god still acting in the human sphere. This prayer did away with abstraction. It gave me a story to cling to, of what God could be. At least I could see clearly what I was up against, brutality and all. This is the mercy of the MRI results. I may not like them, but now I know what we're facing.

Wild West

The small, mewling bundle rustles in its cradle. The second wife doesn't look directly at the baby, staring over the top of his head and into the distance, though the distance is just the sameness of the bare wooden logs that line the cabin walls. She turns away. Disgust lines the ridges of her face.

When it begins to cry she tries to comfort it, but both of them quickly grow distraught. His cries edge towards the frantic when she tries to feed him and when she holds him and when she puts him down. He must sense her distrust, her alarm. His face reddens and he holds his breath, gasps. Silence. Then he wails, louder. *I don't understand him!* she yells. *What does he want?!*

My husband picks him up and rocks him, back and forth, back and forth. He nuzzles the top of his head with his chin.

The second wife must sense the dybbuk's presence within her child. I have heard it said that mothers have a special intuition allowing them to see past the surface of things. A mother knows when her child, miles away, is in danger—when the child has fallen through the surface of an icy pond or gotten its leg trapped under a cart. A mother can feel the breath leave her own body when her child perishes. The cord that once connected her to the child never fully snaps. She can intuit that which cannot be explained by the rational men of the world, defying the physical rules of reality, much like a ghost. A mother already has one foot in the next world; she is more dead than she was before she gave birth, in the time when the baby was contained inside her. The process of untangling the baby from her womb and expelling it into the world brings her flush with the afterlife. She is more dead than her husband and more dead than her childless neighbors, strutting about town flushed with life. To the mother–even a living, breathing one–the boundary between dead and alive has frayed. Cut alongside the cord. The second wife closes her eyes tight. She is letting go of what she expected from her life.

I lean down and sniff the baby's thin neck, the top of its dark-haired head, still misshapen from birth and caked in a yellowy-white crust, but a ghost cannot smell. I can see the inner-baby, my baby, the dybbuk, below the surface of its pink skin. The way the blood runs in tributaries through the small body, the pulsing of uneven breath through its lungs, the beating of its small, fast heart.

The baby's fingernails are long and sharp. It wields them, clawing at the air which contains me. Does it sense its other mother, dead but present even so? I hum a few bars of a melody into its ear. Its nails continue to claw, searching.

Did I hear something? the second wife says, looking suddenly down at the cradle, straight through me. The invisible bind between us only lets her sense a presence; she cannot tell that it is me, the wife-ghost of her husband, the mother-ghost of the baby within her baby. Or she has an idea but it's unformed, a feeling she can't articulate.

I sense that it unsettles her, the feeling and the not-knowing, the way the ground beneath her shifts. She yearns for the time before. Her eyes dart around the room, trying to hold onto things, trying to account for what is there in front of her as though it might van-ish or shift without warning. It's true, I would warn her if I could, the world can vanish without warning. Probably she expected her world to continue as it was after the birth of her child, but instead she is uncertain of everything. Death quivers around her though she remains alive, though her baby was born alive. She bargained up herself without knowing what she was getting into.

What? asks my husband.

I'm not sure, she says. *I thought I heard a noise.*

My husband pokes at the fire. A small burst of blue heat erupts from the coals. He puts down his poker. The edge is sharp, like the blade the midwife used to bleed me, like the baby's nails.

Should we give it a name? my husband asks.

The second wife stares as though he's said nothing. Did she hear him?

Should we give it a name? he repeats.

The baby? she asks, like she's reminding herself that there is a baby here in the cabin with her and the husband who used to belong to me. Reminding herself that she's birthed a child and that she's a mother. She can't go back.

The baby, he says. His tone is inscrutable.

There is a long silence. The second wife closes her eyes. Her lids take a long while to reopen.

For the baby, he says again.

Oh, I don't think that would be right. The second wife shakes her head. *No, I don't think so.* There is a long pause. *Not yet.*

The baby, asleep in the cradle, reaches an arm up, extends a sharp-nailed finger out in the air, clawing at nothing.

Chicago

At the end of a line of tiny babies, each separated by sliding walls and curtains, Jonah lies, larger than the rest, in a rare windowed cove. I am fairly certain this coveted assignment signifies pity at the depth to which we've plummeted in a matter of days, from that early, euphoric anticipation in the delivery room to the plastic cushions of the family meeting room, though the nurses all act pleasantly surprised by our good fortune. *Look,* they say, *look how far you can see from up here! You can sit in this chair and watch the city! You can even see edge of the lake!* But the bustle outside is entirely clinical: lab coats and ambulances and wheelchairs. We see this sliver of world alone.

Outside: the kind of sun whose heat smudges a wet shimmer on cement and burrows into skin. I am stranded in the hospital's tower, this cold, timeless place, while the summer I had been eagerly waiting for ticks by through the windows. The cold/hot dichotomy makes me feel like I'm operating out of synch, keyed to a different tempo than my surroundings.

In ancient Hebrew poetry, there's no real grammatical distinction between past and present. Such ambiguity empowers the reader to determine the course of the narrative, to establish facts—the *a* then *b* then *c* we have all come to expect from our stories. More to the point, it erases the border between is and was and will be. Without proper grounding and context, it's easy to get lost in the narrative, unsure of the order of events or of how much time has passed between *a* and *b*, or if the events of the story have ended or are ongoing. The diagnosis of HIE, like this ambiguous grammar, exists as past tense and present perfect at once. Sometimes it morphs into future tense, a sprawling, many-tentacled thing. It's the event that occurred in the delivery room, undetected, and the injury recorded on the MRI, and also the future for which we have to wait and see.

The big reveal of the MRI is over. Now the days pile up, muddled. Before, the *tohu* v'vohu of those three days turned to four ratcheted up each minute, each second. We grew highly attuned to the moment's passing; the effect was that the four days expanded into a bubble around us. Once the bubble popped, time did not return to its pre-Jonah state. It stretched out, loose and baggy, without consistent shape or structure. Part of me remains stuck in the before-time, the equivalent of a still photograph embedded in a poorly edited film.

The doula at the coffee shop warned the couple, *The hospital will start the clock the minute they admit you. All you get is 24 hours and then they'll push interventions to make you deliver.* She explained that a woman's body often takes longer to birth than the medical establishment cares to admit, that doctors prefer to keep her on an unnaturally rushed schedule, making her contractions and dilation fit their rigid timeline, one best suited to the doctor's calendar and hospital's fear of litigation. It's her right, the doula seemed to say, for this woman and her birth to take up space. Birthing as a real estate endeavor, parents staking out territory. Claim what's rightfully yours, follow your biological destiny! In spite of my skepticism, I saw the allure of this mode of thinking—women for so long shoved to the margins, made to fit into whatever space was left. The doula offered a path of expansiveness. She picked up her cup as though to take a sip but placed it back down on the table. *I've seen it time and time again.* The couple nodded at her, partaking of a secret.

During one of the post-MRI NICU days that pile up like old newspapers at an abandoned home, my mother goes to Target and buys me a bra that can hold the pump flanges in place around my nipples and a purple lunch box and two blue ice packs for transporting milk back and forth in the summer heat, as well as a loose skirt, pants with elastic waistbands that aren't pajamas but could be, and large T-shirts so I won't have to wear maternity clothes anymore—reminders of a former body full with kicking, protruding baby. I didn't realize that I would continue to look so pregnant for an extended time after the birth. My body would continue to take up space, maybe not in the delivery room but after. The doula had been onto something.

When she hands me the shopping bag, it's like I'm standing in the aisle of BuyBuy Baby, not knowing how to know what I need, and there's the sense that a wave might come and tackle all the items on all the shelves and bury me. The things I needed were not contained in the store, but I didn't know it. Now I know what I need— to fast-forward, to move beyond the waiting—but I don't know how to get there. Instead of going forward I'm falling backwards, back to the store, back to the doula in the coffee shop.

My ASL-teacher friend tells me verbs in sign language have no innate tense. They aren't conjugated. Like biblical Hebrew, context or signage (an inserted "now" or "then" at the beginning of a sentence, for example) signifies the "when" of the sentence. One might assume this connotes a cruder language—unconcerned with nuance, communicating only the barest facts of existence, hardly literary. But now I consider disregard for time embedded in the very syntax of the language advanced—an acceptance that things happen not isolated on a timeline, but again and again and again. Recursive. Events aren't discrete moments but a continuous fabric, clinging to the objects of this world, a texture we relive and relive, unendingly, the way centuries of history hover over the present: the water breaking, transition, experiences piling up and rolling forward as a collective unit, as a wave.

Now that we're on the other side of those three days expanded to four, there's no more countdown. We linger. We learn to measure Jonah's progress by his breathing. Around us there's much discussion of why he's taking so long to breathe on his own (is it related to the brain, either its sedation under seizure and pain medication or, worse, to an undetected injury in an area that controls automatic functions?

[The MRI doesn't always catch everything, the doctors have warned.] Or is it due to the thick meconium inhaled in the lungs?). I want it to be because of the meconium, because lungs can heal. The brain can rewire around an injury but the dead tissue itself can't heal; the past can't be undone. What's dead is dead. When the doctors leave the room, Jed and I make ourselves feel better by presenting the case for meconium as the culprit. We try to reassure each other—*it's the logical explanation,* we say. But we know it's all conjecture and the only way forward to is to wait.

At the start of my second trimester, Jed took me to Paris, a belated birthday gift. We ventured out to Versailles on a rainy, gray day. As we departed the city, clouds gathered outside the train windows. The baby was a small protrusion below my navel. I could see it, but few others noticed. Before pregnancy, I had no idea that so many of the 40 weeks would pass before the baby made itself known to the outside world, the fetus cramming those final months with an oversized amount of growth.

We walked from the train station and arrived to gardens tangled over with brown thistles (it was winter), then snaked through room after room of gold filigree, jewel-encrusted bassinets, portraits the size of SUVs. Statues of kings and queens, faces taut, chalky white, lined the hallway. Preserved in stillness.

These post-MRI days have the same stilled quality. Jonah lies statue-like, arms and legs frozen. He looks like he's sleeping but I'm not sure he's capable of sleep, not real sleep, given the powerful drugs that keep him sedated and the underlying chaos that might still bubble beneath. Jed and I are also slowed, robotic. We move through the motions, day after day, sitting bedside, waiting, but we aren't sure for what. We idle in the timelessness, the waiting for Jonah to become ready to move out of statue-dom. Now there is no set timeline, unlike the three turned to four days we started with. Doctors make no promises about where we'll go from here. We have to wait for Jonah to give us a sign, to tell us what he will become, what he's capable of. Will he breathe? Will he eat? Will he walk or talk? Will he see? Will he have a favorite song or book? Will he know me?

Jewish tradition harps incessantly on waiting for the Messiah and the redemption he'll bring. Many modern Jews understand that the Messiah will not come, though prayers speak of that moment. The Messiah will never come because the world will never be perfect. The world will never be perfect because brokenness is one of its preeminent, defining traits; the world would cease to be the world without brokenness and would be something else instead. The world is defined by brokenness because humans depend on it for purpose (this is the irony of grief, that we so desperately need it). Besides, the Messiah itself is the figment of an ancient imagination, rooted in superstition and magical thinking, and now waiting has become the thing itself.

Waiting has become the thing itself in the hospital, too. For the three days, for the MRI results, for Jonah to breathe on his own, for him to eat. With each goal achieved, the goalpost moves around the bend and out of sight. I'm beginning to internalize that the waiting won't stop once we leave the hospital. *Wait and see,* everyone tells us, with cheerful optimism, because it's got to be better than the bleakness of an unblinking prognosis with no hope, right?

When we decide to return to our apartment only a few miles from the hospital, on the same street as the hotel only across a river and highway, we may as well be refugees repatriating to our far-flung village, peering around the bend to glimpse the extent of wreckage left by occupying forces—Romans or Cossacks or Germans or Huns. My parents scrubbed the place in an attempt to rid it of evidence of the before: crumbs left on the counter and toothpaste smears on the sink and pajamas thrown off in a hurry on the way to that final doctor's appointment when I didn't realize I was in labor. Novels now line up neatly along the shelf, bookended with a vase of fresh flowers. The bar of Dove that once sat naked on the tub ledge now nestles in a newly purchased ceramic bowl alongside a twin bar of purple lavender soap, hand-milled. Still, the bassinet stands beside our bed—an abscess. No one knew what to do with it. *Should I put it away?* Jed asks, as though it's infectious, in need of the containment suite. But

I'm not sure the presence of the empty bassinet can touch us. We've reached a saturation of difficulty.

I've moved from hospital to hotel to home and still a part of me is stuck in the vent of the delivery room, always. Is Jed stuck, too? When he looks past me, is it because he's glued to the pull-out bed in the containment room? Is he trying to make his way back to the present? Standing by the fireplace, I can feel the vibration of the arms of lights descending from the delivery room ceiling and the rattle of supply carts when the doctor says it's time to push and that she will only give me two hours because two hours is all the baby can handle. The baby could not handle even that, but we didn't know it then. Jed, pouring coffee in the kitchen, may also be looking over the doctors' shoulders to see Jonah for the first time, gray and misshapen, over and over again.

Wait at home for as long as you can, the doula advised her prospective clients that day in the coffee shop in the before-time, when the days still retained their shape. The doctors could be impatient and wouldn't allow for too much waiting; the couple who rightly prized waiting must do so on their own. Like the Jewish Messiah, a good birth cannot be rushed, she seemed to imply. Good things come to those who wait, or so the saying goes.

At some point the doctors order lower vent settings to give Jonah a chance to show that he can breathe on his own. Then, after he manages on progressively lower settings, they extubate him. Later, nurses switch out his large nasal cannula for a small one, go from much oxygen to less to room air with positive pressure inflating his lungs. His body begins to flinch and flail. There are signs he's there, but it's not a given. Not yet.

Before Jonah I knew nothing of such gradations. A breathing tube was a breathing tube. Now it is the primary language I speak. I pay close attention to the numbers doctors read as they determine next steps, to the reports nurses give about his course overnight, to the bald and wiry respiratory therapist as he replaces one tube with another, hovering over the bed to monitor response, but when I look away for an instant, I lose track of what it's all about, what we're waiting for now.

Jonah opens his eyes. I am not by his bed. I'm in the NICU waiting room talking to a friend who has stopped by for a visit. Behind us, a family unpacks parcels of food—rice and lentils and curries and naan—spoons servings onto paper plates. Cumin and curry waft through the room. *Hurry! Hurry!* Jed yells, from the doorway. *Come quick!* It's like I'm missing the birth of my child. It's my fear from the hematologist's office—of birthing while asleep—come true, except instead of under anesthesia, I'm simply in the wrong place. It's so mundane.

I limp-run down the hall, ignoring the rules of my body and the hospital. Time is suddenly moving in jumps, ecstatic peaks on a chart, irregular and unpredictable. As I near Jonah I'm no longer waiting for anything. All of my energy—mental and physical—is propelled into action.

When I reach the end of the line of babies, I approach the isolette and stare down. Jonah is here. He is a person. He searches the room, taking in all that there is and all that he missed. He's emerging from under water. I'm so happy for him, present finally, and so sad that he is beginning from behind the starting line, that he has to catch up on lost time. For the first time I am looking at another person.

He has such bright blue eyes! the nurse remarks. I didn't think to notice their color. I picture the blue cap that wasn't really blue, the blueness of the sea that held the whale that was really a fish. Jed stands on the other side of Jonah. He takes my hand, not in the way he's been holding it, an attempt to comfort me or him, but victoriously. We stand there, all three of us together.

The Jewish Messiah may be a mercurial, elusive figment of a desperate, ancient imagination, but the Messiah in *Godspell* was no figment. Kinetic, corporeal, he walked and breathed and sang and danced. He jumped to center stage and twirled and sweat dark patches onto his blue Superman tee and whipped the audience into fervent applause. After performances, he sauntered through the linoleum-floored hallways of the church, cracked open sodas purchased from the vending machine, tied his scraggly hair back into a ponytail. He spanned the divine and the human.

The archetype of a messiah is so powerful because it links these two seemingly divided realms. Jesus, of course, is the ultimate crossover, and a play about Jesus takes this to yet another, meta level. The NICU also holds two unlikely realms in tandem. There's the profane—exhausted family members cracking open their own sodas purchased from the waiting room vending machines; nurses discussing their shift schedules; phlebotomists performing arterial sticks; signs listing handwashing protocol—and the holy—the moment a baby opens his eyes for the first time.

Jonah's nurse looks down at her beeping pager. *What is it?* I ask. *A delivery,* she says. *They're requesting a NICU team downstairs. Must be some complication.* I remember the team gathered in my room in the before-time, the crowd of faces I was dimly aware of as the forceps birthed my child. Once again I'm back there, watching them crowd the body.

When she returns, not twenty minutes later, I ask, *Everything ok?* Secretly I hope for some disaster, that another family peers at their child who isn't yet their child, blue-capped, white-brained, cordoned in the Mother/Baby suite at the other end of the hall. It's lonely here, in this place. *Oh, yeah,* she says, as if she's already forgotten the reference. *Fine. Only a precaution.* She turns to check Jonah's monitor. It's started to beep; maybe the IV is out of fluid? She presses a button.

Good, I say, *that's good.* I imagine the happy family, taking their first photos. The mother smelling the top of her baby's head as it lies on her chest. I look at Jonah, open eyes so full of hope and yet I can promise him none of what those parents in that delivery room can promise their babies. I thought we'd reached the saturation point of difficulty, that nothing more could make us go deeper, but there is no such thing. The Jews wait and wait for the Messiah; there is no cap on the waiting. There is no cap on difficulty, on grief.

As if to further prove the point that there's no limit, a new family moves into the bay directly across from Jonah with their son, a boy given a last name as a first and first for last. He's been brought in for some uncomplicated problem. A mild infection or light flutter under the stethoscope has landed him here for observation or antibiotics. *Better safe than sorry,* the doctors and nurses repeat. The bays are only semi-private, separated enough that I don't know the boy's exact diagnosis but not so much that I can't hear what follows.

The boy's parents are not lulled by the matter-of-factness of the staff, who explain that keeping the baby here is standard procedure. *None of this is how we wanted his birth to go,* the mother yells. Maybe they had enlisted the doula from the coffee shop, spent hours planning each step of the delivery process, plotting responses to medical scenarios, reading recommended books, only to have it fall to pieces at the last minute. I take a deep breath but inhale too much of the sticky sweet residue the sanitizing wipes have left on all the surfaces.

You're holding him hostage! the father shouts, demanding the doctors release him against protocol. They've been here too long, and they are sick and tired of waiting, he argues.

They don't understand what waiting is, I think, not really.

He's the healthiest baby in this whole place. Just look around, the father shouts.

Do not listen to those comparisons, I tell Jonah. *They're idiots,* I say. *Bullies. Don't pay attention.*

Jonah pulls my hands from over his ears, straining his head in the direction of the noise. Now that he can see, he wants to take it all in. He's not afraid.

What does one call the person in a sign language conversation who is not signing? I want to ask my friend. It can't be listener. Is there a word for understanding a communication that doesn't rely on the aural? Would that person be a viewer? Absorber? Understander? Receiver? Is this what Jonah is now, eyes open, looking for this other family, for the healthiest baby?

Day after day Jed and I sit and watch Jonah, and when we are given permission, when his stats are stable, we pick him up, pass him back and forth. If I close my eyes, it is almost like holding a baby, except for the smell of hospital. Its chemicals invade the crevices of furniture and the paneled walls and curtains that separate us from the other babies and parents.

Jed goes to work some mornings. *It'll be good to start getting things back to normal,* he insists. *Back to a routine.* He assumes we can rewind to what came before, and that time can resume its normal pace.

Going back to work won't be a distraction, he is careful to point out, but a productive use of his days. *I'm not doing anyone any good sitting here*, he says, motioning around our small NICU bay.

I have no such escape from waiting, from motherhood, and I say I don't want one. I say I need to be here. Mostly it is that I understand I can't return to what came before no matter how much I want it. I wake each morning and rush to pump and shower and drive to the hospital in time for rounds. It doesn't matter that there's rarely any new information doled out.

When the doctors decide he's ready, I attempt to feed Jonah, first from the bottle, then from my breast, but it's a clumsy process, the cords and wires tangling around arms and legs. He tires easily, still shaking off his heavy sedation. The nurses try to prop him up on stiff hospital pillows and show me how to bring his mouth to my breast (*Not the other way around!* they warn, as though something terrible and irreversible will happen if I make that mistake) and with their cold hands they compress my tissue, rhythmic squeezes to make up for his weak muscles. None if it is natural, and the milk does not come easily.

I delay my departure in the evenings because I worry Jonah will wake and I won't be there to hold him and he will know he is alone. I think of missing the moment he opened his eyes. He has spent so much of his short life unconscious, and both of us have no choice but to make up for the lost time. Mostly this means I wait while he sleeps. Time now is unpartitioned, winding, rambling and flabby; it's almost boring here, except that I'm on constant edge and can't let down my guard. I don't know what I'm waiting for exactly that makes me so agitated—there's no more MRI, no more results set to come. It's a general sense of unease, which may be worse; this unease has no endpoint, and so I'm not sure when or if it will relent.

The resurrection is conspicuously missing from *Godspell*, though I read somewhere it's implied by Jesus's return during the curtain call. Otherwise, the play asks the audience to accept a god without his ending. In this way the salvation of *Godspell* is frankly quite Jewish—ongoing, aspirational, grounded in process and not outcome, a tattered flag waving in the distance that no one quite expects to reach. Motherhood, I can see now, from this post-MRI NICU vantage, will be similarly aspirational. The waiting for Jonah to evolve into himself has no end. It may have moments I trick myself into believing will bring closure, but then another hurdle will arise and I'll realize that the waiting is ongoing. We will never achieve safety, salvation. Jonah is a person with open eyes and Jonah is also a process of unfolding.

The yoga teacher recited:
>*Let your brain melt away*
>*let the frontal lobe melt away.*
>*You have nothing to do*
>*and nowhere to go.*

She may have been predicting Jonah's injury, or she may have been speaking of motherhood and its

interminable exile.

When I find Jonah's MRI report buried in his medical records I read it over and over again, until I know it like a prayer. "Other than mild involvement of the posterior lateral thalami, the deep nuclei and brainstem are spared," it says. Each time I get to that line, I inhale—sharp relief. I hold onto it like a child grasping a security blanket. I don't yet know Jonah, he is still unfolding, eyes opening. I am waiting for him, so I cling to this bit of mercy: a part of Jonah's brain has been "spared" from his injury. Here, spared means to be the recipient of incomplete salvation. Plenty of his brain was injured, the report says, but not all. The cap wasn't able to protect everything, but it could be worse, the radiologist seems to imply in the note. Perhaps this is the kind of messiah Jews wait for, if they could ever get past the waiting itself; a savior of stingy sparing rather than of full ascension to a higher plane. Should we give thanks for mere sparing? Does gratitude sanction the initial brutality? Rationalization of the grotesque?

Dr G. visits every few days, between deliveries. *He looks great,* she says, peering at the infant in my arms. Though she is, technically speaking, only a doctor to babies still in that black box of the womb, relinquishing her duties upon their exit, I nod. I will take any assurance of normality.

Jonah looks like a baby. But for the collection of probes emitting vital signs onto the bedside monitor, the cannula in his nostrils, he demonstrates little evidence of the blow. All babies look like babies, spared physical manifestations of their circumstances in these tiniest days. Given time they grow into their pain. Their limbs cannot coordinate movement or their minds and mouths cannot form speech. But new babies should only flail and cry, their state marked by lack of coordination, by chaos—*tohu v'vohu.*

What do you need? Dr. G. asks as she stands to go.

More pads and mesh underwear would be great, I say. *Oh, and maybe another waffle pillow.* The staff on the postpartum floor have blockaded my mother's requests for extra supplies. *There should be enough in the bag we give at discharge,* they say, silently chastising my body for exceeding the allowable limit, as though it should have, long ago, finalized its recovery.

Dr. G. shakes her head: *They're getting stingy for some reason. I'll find a way to get more for you.*

This is her version of a donut. The extension of an offering into an impossible abyss.

She can't undo what's been done. This would be akin to the impossibility of ushering in the Messiah who will never arrive. This would be bestowing a full salvation rather than a sparing. We are stuck in the waiting. But she can offer us this.

Wild West

Time passes; how much, precisely, depends on which side of death time is viewed from. I move in and out of the walls, between the bed and the chest full of linens. I slink into the slats between the floorboards. I float in the rafters, hang alongside the salted meats. I crouch down beside the cradle and watch the still-unnamed (in spite of my husband's questions) and unbaptized (in spite of the preacher's wife's urgings) baby suckling at air in his sleep, his cheeks moving in and out, his lips smacking, the dybbuk trying desperately to break through and speak.

I watch as the second wife struggles to feed the baby, to sate him and get him to sleep soundly. He wakes urgently the moment she places him down—no matter how softly she lowers him into the cradle, no matter how tightly she swaddles him in thick blankets—rooting and red-faced. She must pick him up and begin the process anew.

From my vantage on the ceiling over the bed, her breasts resemble the rolling hills in the landscape outside, only inverted in shade. Instead of red dirt covered in melting caps of snow, these are pale white and laced with blue veins, topped in circles of red. The baby's mouth fumbles against her nipples; he bites down with his toothless mouth and his gums clamp angrily on the white skin. I wonder if the dybbuk can taste the milk, too, from inside the baby, and if it tastes strange to him, foreign.

The second wife winces with each suck. She cries out and stops herself partway through, as though stuffing her own mouth with invisible cloth to stifle the sounds. I can feel her pain in me as though I had her body. I could not feel my own body as the women cleaned it but I can feel hers. This connection between us shocks like a current encased in a glass globe in one of those traveling exhibitions. We are as intertwined as our babes.

The baby shakes his head frantically, searching, between latches. At one point he bites so hard at her breast that a blackish blister forms and when he bites again in the same spot it erupts in a purulent mess. He bites and bites, extracting blood and milk, a pinkish-orange mess, the color of a beautiful sunrise. Tears stream down the second wife's cheeks but she looks more enraged than sad or pained. Startled by, angry at, where she's been deposited. *Just think*, I want to tell her, *that you could have ended up like me. This is nothing, your pain. This is not pain.* But the better angel buried deep in me reminds me that pain is pain is pain. It doesn't translate from person to person, experience to experience. I am ashamed at how quick I am to judge another, even one with whom I share so much—a husband, a home, a child.

Devil, she hisses at the baby as it suckles, clamping down with those sharp gums.

I flinch for a moment, thinking she is speaking to me, that she sees me floating. Then I grow angry, for she must be speaking to what can only be the dybbuk, the sense of alienation she feels from the baby but cannot place. *That is my child you speak of!* I want to shout, but I can't.

You'll heal in time, the midwife tells her when she visits. She leaves an ointment for the wounds on her breasts, greenish and gloppy.

I feel an ache in my breast. I reach for it before realizing I have no breast.

The second wife does not apply the ointment. I watch it sit on the table beside the bed. Once I see her reach for it but pull her hand back as though the jar is too hot. The wound on her breast festers.

My husband continues with his days as before, executing his manly duties. He hunts and skins animals, he collects wood for the fire, he repairs a broken windowpane, he tends to the horses outside, bringing them oats and hay, cleaning a wound on the young one's leg. I don't doubt that he cares for the wife and child, or that he would care if he let himself. But he chooses not to look too closely, at his wife or the baby. I wonder if this is because he thinks of me, if his mind is half stuck on what could have been, on the life that passed by him, on the dead. I think there may be a slow sadness to his lumbering step but I have been known to interpret things selfishly before, to assume they were about me when they weren't.

Devil, the wife continues to hiss at the baby as it sucks.

My husband, succumbing to the preacher's wife's urging, asks the second wife if they should get the baby baptized. She pushes off the question. This would entail naming him, of course, laying claim to this child she does not believe is hers. *When he's older,* she says. Or she pretends not to hear him, clanking the pots in the hearth, beating the rug with particular fervor. She worries also, I think, about what it would mean to bless something possessed, to bless the devil, that she would somehow be inverting the order of the world.

Sometimes she spits when she curses at the baby, a foam forming at the corners of her mouth like a rabid dog, such is her rage. I worry she might throw the baby, that she might smack it on the ground or against the wall. Would I be able to intervene to save it? Is there anything that might allow me to break free of the bonds of death and act in the world? Perhaps the second coming the preacher promised as he paced his makeshift altar, when bodies and souls would reunite, but I didn't believe in that in the first place, let alone now.

One morning the second wife grows frustrated with the endless sucking and pulls her breast away, so suddenly it causes the baby's head to whip to the side. The child cries out. The second wife shouts at it—*Stupid ingrate! Demon spawn!* Then, more sadly, hopelessly: *What in god's name do you want from me?*

The baby roots, trying to latch again. It cares not at all about the second wife's cruel utterances. The second wife gives in. She looks tired, forlorn. The baby suckles. In its hunger it leaves the second wife's breasts no time to heal. The same wound still festers. The dybbuk must be looking for something it hasn't found.

It pains me to watch as it searches and searches and does not find what it seeks. Sometimes the baby cries out, sometimes he grows tired of crying and stares blankly, desperately alone. I try to appreciate the beauty of the baby's cheeks, the deep crackle in his eyes, the sweep of his hair, some part of which belong to my dybbuk son cloistered inside this foreign body. But the experience of beauty is tempered. There is nothing like the guilt of a mother who can only watch her child suffer. And then watch the suffering turn into nothingness, a resignation.

Still, I cannot leave. I am compelled to stay, though I cannot do anything to help him. I am helpless. I must witness him, must watch him. The act of watching, of keeping watch, is enough to keep me tethered.

While I wait—I'm not sure for what, for my dybbuk son to grow?—I keep watch, too, over my baby's brain preserved in the jar at the doctor's. I move seamlessly between the homes. The doctor removes it daily and peels and slices the tissue, hunching over it, unable to take his eyes off of the grooves of tissue. He is delicate with the brain, careful not to disturb it more than his examinations require. He places the parts back together when he is finished, when his candle is burnt to a stub. He speaks to it sometimes in a low voice, almost a cry, like a penitent. The doctor and the brain are as linked as me and the second wife.

Chicago

No longer cordoned in our euphemistic suite, we have NICU neighbors on the other side of our sliding glass wall. The mother with stringy blond hair and bright red toenails atop swollen feet stops me at the hall sink as I wash my pump equipment with the silver packets of Castile soap that won't sud no matter how much I scrub, and tells me how, a year before, she gave birth to a stillborn girl who had stopped growing—suddenly, inexplicably—in the womb. She rushes to get the story out, like the words are coals burning her mouth and she must expel them to stop the singe.

Months later, she continues, she became pregnant, this time with twin boys who, like their sister, also ceased to grow. She demanded an immediate C-section against medical advice. Too soon, the doctors warned. They tried to convince her to wait. *But I couldn't live with myself if it all happened again*, she tells me.

The babies had been in the NICU for many weeks before we arrived. One boy had grown well, got discharged home; the other lagged behind. At some point he contracted a fungal infection his body couldn't fight.

We called in our priest, the mother says, tugging at her stringy blond hair. *Said last rites. Thought it was goodbye*. She cannot look directly at me. She stares at her feet. Somehow the boy pulled through, though doctors warned only time would reveal the full effects of his ordeal. Each breath she takes during the pauses of her story tremors. I imagine the baby's brow glistening, anointed, waiting for the priest's blessing.

But this is not my story. The mother with red toenails recounts the arc of her sons' lives, and also her daughter's life, which never came to fruition, all of which now eclipse her entire life up until this point. She asks me about Jonah, but his narrative sits in lumps that dissolve as soon as I try to pick them up.

One day, I might say to her, *my son kicked my ribs. The next he could only breathe through a blue plastic tube.* I can't explain how one statement—one state of being—connects to the other.

Each morning after the objects of the room take shape around me, somehow both intrinsically the same as before and unspeakably altered, I prompt myself: *Put your feet on the floor, walk to the bathroom, turn on the shower, climb in.*

The shower is the most difficult place for me to be. The cascade of water delivers a suffocating sadness. I am alone and without distraction; the shower is so ordinary and yet I feel foreign in it. Sometimes Jed comes in to shave or brush his teeth and I feel a momentary respite in his company, in the sound of him spitting into the sink. The two of us have grown even closer in the last few weeks as the outside world has ebbed further out of reach. We share an experience no one else can fathom, no matter how hard they try, and still, he wasn't in the delivery bed when the doctor took out the forceps, he isn't the body who asphyxiated the baby. A gap remains and there's no way to bridge it. Unlike infants, we have fully developed theories of mind—we understand that we are not the same person.

After showering and dressing, we go to the NICU, nodding at the other mothers and fathers as we pass each other on our way to our babies. Mostly we don't speak. Occasionally one I recognize from the waiting room will utter a soft hello, trying to reach out into the space between. We have so much in common and yet share so little.

My children cause me the most exquisite suffering of which I have any experience, writes Adrienne Rich.

Adrienne, I want to scold, *do you know you speak in hyperbole?*

But, of course, I have no idea of her suffering, of its scope or depth or how long the pain lingered or if it ever left at all.

Standing beside the mother of twins, red toenails poking up out of her sandals as she rehashes her story, it seems everyone else had a warning shot, an explanation—and this, I imagine, makes their fates easier to swallow. Pictures of premature babies glued to hot air balloon cutouts hang on the wall in the family room, captioned with success stories: *Born at 2 pounds, now I love hot dogs and swimming and my new sister!* My baby is not premature or small; his illness fissures delicate tissue below the surface. Blinded by my pain, I cannot see this woman's small, still baby girl carried in her mind's eye while pushing a lone twin in his stroller to visit his weaker brother. My compassion, like my son, deflated, compressed by a difficult labor.

Here in the NICU, I am becoming hardened by my own grief, by my self-pitying wallows in the shower each morning. Before I'd assumed personal suffering would increase empathy through proximity; to know pain would be to hold grace for others in pain. That seemed intuitive and natural. I hadn't suffered much—not really, in the scheme of things—so the notion was purely theoretical. Now, though, I automatically assume my experience sits outside the realm of others', that my own trials are levels of magnitude worse, and that I am therefore more martyr than they. Jonah's birth has unearthed a quiet selfishness, a haughty sense of righteousness I am only dimly aware of, coursing beneath the hard shell of pain. Maybe this is fine when it comes to the father yelling that his son is the healthiest child in the NICU, but it's more uncomfortable when faced with the mother of a stillborn daughter.

Later I find I've underestimated my compassion. I hear my NICU neighbor padding around her son's bay, arranging him for a feed, and know, suddenly and with a quiet shock, that her stillborn baby girl hovers, will always hover, as she nurses and diapers and bathes the others. I understand she now parents three children: one at home, one in the hospital, one a ghost.

Contemporary thinkers have a way of presenting life in terms of great internal struggle, borne, perhaps, out of the relative lack of dire circumstances in modernity. Like the natural birthing movement, they're too removed from true suffering. *Return*, I want to say, *to an era when struggle retained physical meaning, when the next meal hinged on deer stalked through a shadowy forest or berries gathered under blazing sun.* Or, millennia later, coins dropped into children's palms after factory shifts, counted out by their mothers to buy a loaf of bread or bottle of milk. Gnawing hunger subsumes interiority and, with it, grief. I think of Maslow's hierarchy of needs.

But I may have gotten it all wrong. Maybe the mother of the factory workers wakes one night to tumble of fire through their crowded tenement building. She escapes with her boy, sandy-haired, ashy arm protruding from a gray, torn shirt, but her smaller daughter lies curled floors above, the connecting stairway consumed by flame. Maybe the lurch of her soul descends onto her hunger pains—which are by now a wide and humming constant—deepening the pit. I know by now that there's no saturation point for suffering, it tunnels deeper and deeper, so why should it be any different for her? Why can't hunger and grief coexist? Maslow was wrong.

He's mad, the nurse says, when she pokes Jonah with a needle to draw blood for a newborn screening he's failed, though doctors have reassured us—*do not be alarmed*—it's likely a false positive, something to do with the IV nutrition Jonah received in his early days. Of course I don't believe them. Of course I'm alarmed. I listened to Dr. G. when she gave the same warning and look where it got me. *Screening,* they say, to emphasize that the test catches excess in its net. This time they will be right and we won't be on the side of fluke, but that will take days to emerge.

The nurse can't get the blood. Jonah's veins have curled up from too many prods, burrowing deeper under the skin. She pokes again. *It's good that he's mad,* she says, *we want him to be mad.* Response to pain cannot be taken for granted. There is neurological numbness and emotional numbness. Here we are talking of the neurological. But, truly, is there a distinction? Was the numbness I felt towards the red-toed mother emotional? Or was it neurological? The result of over-identifying with my child, of feeling my own neural capacity bombarded as though I'd also been inundated with the sparks of his seizures? Either way, neurological or emotional, my capacity was overloaded—a dated circuit board retrofitted for a modern building.

Babies and small children don't understand themselves as separate from their caregivers. The boundaries are fluid. Psychologists say theory of mind, that ability to think about the consciousness of another, develops gradually over many years. When a young child feels sadness, they assume their mother does, too, and the reverse applies. If they see their mother sad, they feel it themselves, as though the emotion is theirs. This is an empathy so expansive it collapses into selfishness. At some point, empathy jumps over from a deep well of compassion into a self-serving indulgence. An empathy where a person feels so deeply intertwined with the object of empathy that they become the central subject of the suffering. Motherhood is an exercise in walking the tightrope between expansive and collapsed empathy. The baby is made partly of the mother, comprised of some of her DNA, and so to feel for one's baby means to feel for both another being and oneself, coiled up into a single entity. It's evolutionary to care about the propagation of one's own genetic line, and it's also self-sacrificing. The paragon of a mother is someone who would throw herself in front of a car to save a child. In doing so, though, she's only superficially sacrificing herself. She's saving her child, which means she's also saving herself. No one assumes she'd do the same for a stranger's child. Her empathy stems from understanding that her child is a part of her. The two impulses—self-sacrifice and self-preservation—aren't mutually exclusive.

The yoga teacher commanded us to curve our backs to make room for our babies. *The womb is a safe space, a place of peace,* she reminded the room. At the end of class she told us to curl into a fetal position so we could feel the same peace our babies felt, snug embrace of tissue and heat. We could learn to become good parents by practicing this connection, her chant suggested.

In trying to explain brain plasticity—the remarkable ability of a child to grow new neural pathways around the boulders and ravines carved out by injury—the neurologist describes the inverse, the ways the brain can shrivel and injure itself in the absence of physical trauma. He explains that the MRIs of children raised in Romanian orphanages bear marks of actual injury, similar to Jonah's MRI, due to neglect—babies left to cry in soiled metal cribs, no one to comfort them. Rather than instill hope, this terrifies. There are so many more ways I can harm Jonah. Infinite, apparently!

In response, I am more hesitant to spend time away from the hospital. *Look,* my mother says, *look at that baby in the incubator.* She points across the hall. *Have you ever seen anyone hold her?* She's trying to get me to go home at night, to eat and sleep and drink a dark beer, which the nurses assure me will increase my still-meager milk supply. She means to show me I will do no harm by leaving my baby. But the dismal fates of others don't convince. Now that I've unearthed my latent difficulty extending compassion, I'm more vigilant. I don't want to participate in the dismal game of ranking babies, not according to severity of illness or depth of love for them or whatever other markers we might assign. I don't want to let my own pain numb me to the pain of others.

Aside from all this, the guilt and the fear, my insistence on sitting vigil is also remnant of a pregnancy that has not resolved despite a baby out in the world. The water breaks and breaks and breaks again. Erikson might have said our chemical exchange had been severed weeks before, in the delivery room, but he would have been wrong.

Wild West

The baby grows. It grows and grows and, with it, so does the dyb-buk. I can see bits of him peeking out: in the baby's eyes, a mischie-vous glint; the wide span of his toes as he stretches his body; the high-pitched curl at the end of his screams. I wonder if, as he grows, the dybbuk will be able to see me, if he will recognize me.

One chilly morning as spring settles into the land, the second wife sets out from the house with a basket on her waist. She has left the baby alone inside the cabin, settled in its cradle and pulled beside the fire (ostensibly for warmth, but I wonder if she doesn't wish for a rogue spark to jump out from the flames). She walks alone to the icy stream that runs behind the cabin. It has begun to defrost but crys-tals still cling to the surface in places. She kneels and dips garments from the basket in the cold, clear water, sloshing them about reck-lessly. I recognize my husband's gray woolen socks, the blue blanket I knit for our child before our deaths. She must work fast before her hands grow numb.

When the second wife is midway through the basket, the jail-er's wife walks up from behind, hair gusting in the wind, new blue bruise swelling on her left cheekbone. I only truly knew her after my death. Before she had been but a figure spotted from a distance, someone I felt a haughty pity for, though had never spoken to. Now, though, I consider her amongst my closest companions—a sister. I would like to apply a salve to her bruise, especially to the bro-ken skin along the edges of the mark. To ease her pain, though her expression displays no sign of discomfort. I can tell there is great pain buried deep beneath the skin's surface. She is upbeat in spite of her predicament—the bruises hidden beneath her high-necked blouse that I can see through, the roiling anger that waits for her daily at home. She is the recipient, it seems, of all that her husband cannot expend on his prisoners.

Morning, she calls out to the second wife.

The second wife looks up from her sloshing and nods. Nowadays she hardly speaks. The fact of the dybbuk must be becoming harder to deny. The baby babbles and laughs and she looks through it as though the sounds are utterly alien. I watch her go through the motions of care, changing the baby's soiled clothes, washing the crust that gathers in the folds of its neck, but that's all they are—motions. There is no expression underlying her acts. She does not speak to the baby. If our husband is out, she lets the babe wail for hours on end. She doesn't appear bothered in the slightest by the sound. She does no more than what is absolutely required. If I could, I would reach out and add tenderness to her motions and replace the rough rag she uses for his bath with a softer one, would hold the baby against me when he cries out.

The jailer's wife kneels at the bank beside the second wife. She begins to hum something low and deep. I recognize the melody but cannot place it. Were I still living I would be able to name the song, of this I am certain. The two women wash and wring and rise to hang the clothes and linens from tree limbs near the bank. I think of the convicts hanging at the town gallows, the puff of their clothes in the wind which creates the illusion of life. The sun is crisp and pale, filtered through the first buds that spring out from the ends of the branches.

You've got a little one now, is that right? The jailer's wife asks.

Yes, says the second wife.

How old?

The second wife looks down. She pauses. I think she cannot remember how long it's been. *Many months now*, she says, finally.

Healthy and happy?

He's fat, says the second wife.

The answer seems to puzzle the jailer's wife. Her mouth twitches. *Fat is good*, the jailer's wife says. *You wouldn't want a weak one.*

The second wife does not react. Not even with a glance or a nod. She would, I presume, prefer a weak one. It would be a relief if the child would die rather than thrive with this unknown creature within it. This stranger's child.

I'm with child, my first, says the jailer's wife, pulling her dress taut over her abdomen to reveal a bulge previously hidden under the thick fabric. I remember my womb, in a way. I cannot remember the feeling of the baby pushing against it, but I remember the glee with which I met the jabs, the sense of magic at the transformation occurring under my skin. Previously my body had done nothing miraculous. *Two more months or so.*

God be with you both, says the second wife, her voice, like her face, flat and disinterested. Lately she does not change her tone, no matter what she is saying or to whom. To hear her speak is to listen to a book being droned out, line after dull line, at the schoolhouse. She could speak of an earthquake destroying the entire village and her voice would drone on in the same way as if she were speaking of scrubbing the floors.

I'm not afraid, says the jailer's wife. She absent-mindedly strokes the bruise on her cheek. *Things will either turn out well or poorly. Either way, it is what it is. I've seen what this can mean*, she gestures towards her belly. *It's not always gentle or kind, but at least there's an end.* She looks at the water, the ice crackling as the stream dribbles on. *That's something, to meet one's end.*

The second wife yanks the blue blanket I made for the baby out of the water and wrings it out between her hands. The color has faded, or I've forgotten the shade. She quivers. Does she know I made the blanket? Does she know that the jailer's wife cared for my body? Perhaps she has heard people whisper about my fate, about what happened on that day and the ones that followed. She scoops up the basket without a word. She walks quickly, her heavy breasts shaking. The blisters have mostly healed as she has resisted the baby's cries, but some of the tenderness remains. I follow. She walks so fast she's out of breath. I feel her shaking through the air between us. Something the jailer's wife said has unnerved her.

Goodbye! the jailer's wife yells out. But the second wife is already far in the distance and if she hears, she pretends not to.

At home the second wife puts a blue cap on the child's head, hot and damp from so long near the fire, pulls the string until it splits the babe's chin into two equal blossoms of fat. She yanks it tighter and tighter, trying to lay claim to it, to force out the invader, until she can pull no more. The baby doesn't cry; he has a look of resoluteness to him. The second wife ties a neat bow, double knots the end. She's so frantic she barely seems to notice how low I am floating, how if I were in a body I would almost touch the hairs on her arm.

She holds the baby out away from her and stares at it, as though daring the dybbuk to show itself. She lifts the baby up over her head. She moves it side to side. She places it down on the ground and shines a candle to its face. The baby stares back, silent and unblinking.

Chicago

When the oxygen cannula in Jonah's nose comes out, he relocates once again, this time across the NICU to the wing for the tubeless. The transition occurs when we take a break from his bedside—to the vending machine in the waiting area or through the hospital's tubes and tunnels to buy a sandwich. There's no fanfare. He exists in one place one moment, in another the next.

In this new area, babies writhe, cry out in hunger, fist and unfurl their hands. No one needs permission to scoop them up from their bassinets, to hold them or feed them or change a diaper. On this side of the NICU nurses care for three, sometimes four, infants at a time. I'm not used to the freedom of parenting under such light supervision. Often, I step outside of our pod and search for a nurse, any nurse, to ask: *Is it time for a feed? Should I change his diaper?*

You don't need to ask, they remind me, trying to hide their exasperation. *He's your baby.*

When we're lucky, we get the nurse who cared for Jonah during his days in the cap, who stood beside us when the MRI results came in. She coaxes us through this stage of parenting, too, with no hint of impatience. She parents us while we parent Jonah and often I wonder what we will do without her, whenever we are discharged. I worry I've become dependent on her and that, without her, I'll find myself stuck back in one of Erikson's earlier stages of development—a toddler somehow left to care for a baby.

Here, parents smile and chatter, count days until discharge. They are not waiting for damning diagnoses. Here, we get to bathe Jonah. We dip towels in a tub of warm, sudsy water and dab his skin, careful not to press too hard. With a plastic-bristled brush made for the quaintly normal cradle cap, we instead unfurl glue that stubbornly clings to his scalp from EEG electrodes. Before, in the other wing, they tried to soften the residue with baby oil but only succeeded in slicking his hair back in dark whorls against his scalp. Still his head behind the ears is swollen—maybe from the cooling cap or the injury or some combination of the two. We rinse and rinse again.

Through pregnancy I feared some menacing force (contaminated food, undetected genetic anomaly all too common in Ashkenazi Jews, asymptomatic but dire infection) would invade my uterus and corrupt my child. There was superstition at play, an anxious magical thinking; if I worried about the thing, then I might prevent it from coming to pass. Jed, ever the calm optimist, felt certain all would go smoothly. When I accidentally ate a forbidden food, he comforted me with his quick and certain denial that anything bad would happen; he wouldn't entertain the idea and so neither should I. We'd go back to watching *Breaking Bad* on a laptop propped on his knees in bed, and I would try to emulate his certainty. Still, when the doctor made his pronouncement while I lay in the delivery bed after Jonah was whisked away, or later, when the neurologist read the MRI results, we both plummeted. No previous worry inoculated me against the shock; no intrinsic calm inoculated him. *This means you're already great parents*, our favorite NICU nurse says, of our pain. But I fear it's easier for her to say something, to assign meaning, rather than sit silently and watch.

When my birthday rolls around, Jed and I walk down the street to the donut shop with the pink and white striped awning and choose an assortment of glazed and chocolate and cream to leave in the nurses' lounge, still counting on the donut karma to come through, to change our outcome, to bestow favor on our child.

Jewish folklore holds that Adam's apocryphal first wife, Lilith, had a penchant for stealing newborn babies from their beds. Centuries ago, people took all sorts of precautions to ward off this vengeful woman, employing amulets and red ribbons and spells to protect their children. If they created enough protective barriers, they might outwit the demon. If I buy enough donuts, I too might be able to stop Lilith in her tracks.

My new identity is less mother than it is gambler, dealmaker. My bargaining is retroactive, too. *I would have chosen a c-section and hemorrhaged if it would have spared him,* I tell Dr. G at one of her visits, after she explains why she did not order surgery.

I can handle motor delays, I announce to Jed, *but not cognitive.*

I'll take seizures, I say to the neurologist, when he stops by the new wing to check on Jonah, tap a wand on his toes and shine a penlight into his eyes, *over disability.* Then, later, when I understand what I've offered up, that seizures can liquify what seemed solid, I rescind: no, no, anything but seizures. I lay out what I can and can't handle, but no one's been empowered to bargain with me, not the doctors, and certainly not the removed, Jewish god.

Rationally I know none of this bartering matters—that's not the way the world works—but why not try? Pascal's wager applies this logic to faith; a person might as well believe, because there are only upsides to believing and only downsides to not. The downside here is obvious, though; I might trick myself into thinking I'm responsible for more than I can control. If a Jewish woman failed to procure an amulet against Lilith, and her baby did not make it, did she blame herself? Did she ever overcome the guilt? Will I?

Magic also abounded in the medieval Christian world. Scholars recently determined that women wore parchments known as birthing girdles during pregnancy and delivery. These girdles contained prayers and religious imagery thought to form a kind of protective armor to guide them through danger. One of the manuscripts the scientists analyzed connects wearing the girdle to a happy outcome: *If a woman travel with chylde gyrdes thys mesure abowte hyr wombe and she shall be delyvyrs wythowte parelle.* Protestants, including American Puritans, dismissive of such magical devices and incantations, emphasized that birth, whatever the outcome, manifested

God's will. Now, playing at my own game of dice, I'm not sure which approach I prefer—the puritanical route that absolves the individual of responsibility (it's all in God's hands, fate is predetermined), or the medieval and magical, which, however fanciful, at least gives the illusion of agency.

On the phone, friends say: *Jonah is lucky to have you as his parents.* I'm unsure of many things but I am sure luck has nothing to do with this. It's the puritanical approach sneaking in and overriding the magical thinking; Jonah and me and Jed were not thrown together by some act of fate. We are not meant to be, and we have no say in what comes next. It's all random.

Luck carries two different if connected meanings, depending on use. Luck can be either mathematical or moral. One type encompasses the notion of randomness, of statistical chance. This luck is dispassionate. It is neither intrinsically good nor bad; it simply is. It's the luck of a coin toss, of a random, computer-generated set of numbers. Then there's luck as in lucky, as in to break a leg, as in fingers crossed. This luck means *good*. It's a state of being or a hopeful striving for an imagined outcome. You can turn this kind of luck into its opposite by adding the word "bad."

We have experienced both kinds—really all three—wrapped in one. Jonah's injury was an anomaly, unexpected personally but not statistically, not if you examine the probabilities; it had to happen to someone somewhere—I had just stupidly, selfishly really, assumed it would not be us. We were also deeply unlucky to find ourselves in that small fraction of bad outcomes and, now that Jonah has pulled through, is off the vent, is breathing and seeing and moving, we are, perhaps, maybe, ever so slightly lucky, as in good luck. There remains a part of me that finds even the lucky piece unlucky, the part of me that has not signed up for this sort of parenting and would like a do-over, the part of me who is hesitant to use Jonah's name. Each day that I lock eyes with Jonah that feeling grows more remote, but it does not leave entirely and I worry it may never.

The family with the healthiest baby has by now disappeared from the unit. I didn't see them go but I do see their berth emptied of all signs of their presence, as though they were never there to begin with, slate wiped clean. *He's gone*, I tell Jonah. *You don't have to worry about him anymore.* I hated them for their callousness, but also for their luck. They existed in contrast to our luck. They were a version of us if we had fallen on the other side of the probability line. They didn't know it, though; they thought they were unlucky, stuck in the NICU for a small, silly reason, against their will and in contradiction with their birth plan. Luck is in the eye of the beholder.

Before the modern era, women's lives centered around reproduction. With only unreliable folk remedies for contraception, women easily found themselves stuck in a near-constant cycle of pregnancy, delivery, and postpartum recovery. Each time their own safety was far from guaranteed. Some pregnancies resulted in live babies. Some in stillbirth or miscarriage or abortion. Some babies came out sick or died in infancy. Bad outcomes (a deformed fetus, for instance) were often attributed to divine retribution. This is, of course, different from luck. Divine retribution is about just dessert: bad people getting bad things. In spite of myself it's tempting to take on this kind of thinking. Not in some rational way—I have sinned and so this is what God has wrought—but via a primal disgust with my body. I flinch when Jed reaches out to touch me, a kind touch, to let me know he is there, really there. That he hasn't forgotten about us in all of this. I flinch because I don't want to inhabit the thing that failed me and Jonah, the thing that must be rotten, and Jed's touch is a reminder that I do and I can't escape it.

From bed I call the NICU late at night. If I don't call I worry my delinquency will usher in some awful outcome. Karma lurks. Constant vigilance!

The receptionist puts me on hold, pages the nurse. I wait five, ten minutes for a voice on the other end. Each time, the delay, the silence and stillness, is a version of waiting for the MRI results, the feeling of my future and Jonah's future (at this point, the same) hanging in the balance. *How's he doing?* I ask when the nurse picks up, my breast pump whirring in the background. I try to make my voice sound calm and collected. And then comes the torrent of questions: *Is he sleeping? How much milk did he get through his tube? Was he able to swallow from the bottle? Is he maintaining his oxygen saturations? Did the results from his lumbar puncture come back from the lab? Or do we need to wait until morning, or another day, or two, or three?* Hospitals don't distinguish between nights and days and neither do infants. Dark or light they wake and sleep and eat and cry while machines hum and test results populate charts. There's no time to let my guard down.

Jed sleeps next to me. When I finish gathering my data, I tap him and whisper the findings in his ear and he shrugs. He doesn't remember any of it in the morning. His body, somehow, can sleep solidly through the night and resume its crouched waiting in the morning. This is one of the ways that the gap between us persists. I am thoroughly enmeshed in our new reality, in sleep and while awake. I live in my faulty body and so there's no respite.

"First demonstration of social trust in the baby is the ease of his feeding, the depth of his sleep, the relaxation of his bowels," writes Erikson. "The experience of a mutual regulation of his increasingly receptive capacities with the maternal techniques of provision gradually helps him to balance the discomfort caused by immaturity of homeostasis with which he was born." The mother mediates the baby's relationship with the world. Without a mother, what is a baby to do? Maybe this is why I can't let go, even for a night's sleep.

Once he breathes on his own for 72 hours with no desats, we can talk discharge, the nurse explains, tap tapping away at the keyboard. *We're finally at the point where that's all we have left. Last hurdle.*

Great! Jed says. He leans over the crib. *Time to come home, buddy.*

Only 72 hours? I ask. I'm afraid of leaving the hospital, of parenting on our own, in the real world.

But if he desats we go back to start, the nurse warns. *The clock resets. NICU regulations.*

We begin to count, eyes fixed on the screen with his oxygen reading.

When the neurologist refers to my womb as a black box, he means that there's no way to know exactly what was going on inside it, and also, perhaps, that this is pregnancy's version of random luck. Another way to think of it: the womb as a magic eight ball, shaken until a small snippet gets revealed. Everything else inside remains hidden.

Luck is everywhere and luck is a black hole that cares nothing for anyone or anything. In theology this leads to theodicy, the problem of evil. What kind of god would cause an innocent baby to suffer? Is it a god we care to worship? Why did Job stay constant in his devotion in spite of his meaningless, ongoing suffering, in spite of being an unknowing token in some silly game between God and Satan? In the wake of this problem arises superstition. I didn't consider having a baby shower when I was pregnant; Jews have long believed that such premature celebration attracts the evil eye—the ayin hara. I didn't actually believe in the evil eye, waiting to punish me for arrogance, but the notion was somehow deeply embedded anyway. As though years of my ancestors' worries, their superstitious spitting three times to ward away the ayin hara, had snuggled itself into my modern, empirical DNA.

One night I forget to call the NICU. I wake in the morning to sun streaming in through our south-facing windows, almost blinding. I panic. It's like I've forgotten to do the requisite spitting three times to ward off the bad. *It's fine*, Jed tells me. *He's fine. You don't need to call.*

Am I your mother? I ask Jonah, upon arrival later that morning. I've missed his feed in addition to the call and the nurse has given him his bottle, moments before; he closes his eyes and begins to sleep. All day I wait for something bad to happen. I've slipped up, forgotten to utter my spell and given Lilith an opening. When nothing happens, I wait some more.

In those first days after delivery, the hospital walls were thick enough to mute the clamor of July Fourth outside, the fireworks at the lake, the tourists screeching drunkenly, but we could still hear some of the explosions and see the flashes of color cascading over the water. Someone (a nurse? a phlebotomist?) joked that we'd always have a party ready for Jonah's birthday. *A built-in celebration! How lucky for him!* I felt suffocated by everyone's desire to ascribe luck to us, the decidedly unlucky. To untangle luck, winch it out of thick mud like it's some half-dead, mangled fish. Did they believe this labeling could bestow good fortune, willing the phenomenon into being? It's not that different, on its face, from giving the middle name "Chaim," but one came from me and Jed, trying to grab back the harnesses that have slipped through our palms, and the other from near strangers flitting in and out, doing their jobs while trying to dodge the darkness that bore down, trying to escape the vacuum pull of the containment room.

We make it three days, again. It's time. Jonah's discharge from the hospital takes the form of a checklist. Each item neatly typed with a box beside it to indicate completion. This time, birth is bureaucratic.

We've been in the hospital long enough to have a new batch of residents on the unit. When the team rounds, I recognize someone I know from home, from childhood, an old friend of my sister's. It's been decades but still I retrieve her name from the recesses. *How funny!* we say, laughing. *What a coincidence! What are the odds?*

The attending doctor (it's a weekend and a new one we've never met is on call in spite of attempts at continuity) examines Jonah and tells us: *He looks good. He's eating. He's gaining weight. He's breathing without incident.* The bar, I realize, is low. *I'll sign the papers and you can go,* he declares. *There's no more reason to keep him here.*

I understand this to translate as: there is nothing more we can do for him here. You have to wait and see. We are butting up against the limits of medical knowledge.

What do we watch for? we ask.

What would you watch for on a normal baby? the doctor replies, as though the question is an answer. The truth is I have no idea.

Enjoy your baby, the doctor says. The team shuffles out, toward the next patient.

Our favorite nurse, the gentle one, has made sure to work today, our projected day of discharge. She helps us strap Jonah into his car seat, mimicking the way she lovingly taped his breathing tube to my collar bone after the three days of cooling so I could hold him for the first time. She checks to make sure the harness is tight enough, that the chest clip is pulled up to the right place, unnaturally high at the armpits.

She hands us a stack of papers with a prescription for his seizure medication, pages of instructions on how to safely bathe and swaddle and feed a baby, warning signs for infection and illness and ways to spur newborn development, and lists of follow-up appointments where they will test for disorders no one has yet mentioned. She walks us to the interior elevator labeled STAFF ONLY, then down the empty back hallways until we are spit out at the drive at the front of the hospital, beside the red-vested, singing doorman. This is discharge protocol.

There are now more moments of birth than I can count. Delivery and naming and the first time I held Jonah and the day he opened his eyes and the discharge checklist and crossing the threshold into our car, from the nurse's care to ours, and more in between I've lost track of. No matter how many times he's born he still does not seem completely mine. Maybe this time it will stick?

We click the car seat into its base. I don't trust that it's secure. We wave goodbye to the nurse, turn one corner and another. I'd like to reverse the car and drive back to her but I'm sitting beside Jonah to make sure he doesn't stop breathing. Jed drives very slowly. At red lights, he glances up at us in the rearview mirror. I don't talk. I focus my attention entirely on Jonah. If I do this job well enough, maybe this time I can protect him. There's no more magic to turn to, no protective spell to utter. I've already said the words of the Mi Shebeirach with the Rabbi before the MRI and gambled away cerebral palsy for epilepsy. I've exhausted the options. Now there's just me. I can't let my guard down.

Wild West

It's late evening when my husband comes home, and the second wife begins to dress herself to go out. She puts on a layer of britches and one of our husband's flannel shirts, followed by a dress, then an overcoat and a bonnet. She shoves one of our husband's hats in a satchel, along with a brown vest and a flask and some coins she has stashed away in a small box under the bed. All afternoon I have watched her pace the cabin while the baby cried out, then grew tired from its cries and slept, only to wake and begin the cycle again. The second wife is restless. Something about her encounter with the jailer's wife has made her more distressed than before. Her eyes narrow when she looks towards the baby, so sharp they might pierce the skin. I worry for him.

Where are you headed at this time of night? our husband asks. I am beginning to think of him as hers, too, from so much time spent watching the two of them together. I do not know if this is a gesture of generosity or resignation.

I told a friend I would meet her at the inn, she lies. *I won't be out long.*

You can't walk by yourself, not all the way to town in the dark, our husband protests, but not strongly. He is tired, his voice weak. He sinks into a chair by the hearth. It's been a long day. I know because every day is long here, and hard. It's late but the sun clings to the horizon. It's stubborn, like all of us on the frontier.

I'll take the horse, she says. *And a pistol, if you want. There are beans for you, in the pot. Still warm. He should sleep until I get back.* She gestures towards the cradle where finally the child seems to have settled into a long slumber. Our husband takes off his shoes, begins to scrape the mud out from between the grooves in the soles with his nail.

I watch her guide the horse, lamp in one hand to light the way, along the rocky pathway and enter town. There she hitches it to the posts between the tavern and darkened post office. She sidles past the open doors of the tavern and looks in for a moment. A rowdy huddle of men, unshaven, shirts untucked, faces dirt-streaked, slam their cards down on the table in front of them so hard the wood might crack in half. Coins jingle in the center. Probably she has never seen so much money at once. She watches in the darkness as the men hoot and slam and paw at the coins. Sometimes one sweeps them off the table into a palm; sometimes one rises from the table empty handed, head hung, punching a fist into the vacant, boozy air.

The second wife goes behind the building and takes off her coat and dress to reveal the pants and shirt beneath, pats the pistol tucked deep in the pants' pocket. She takes out the vest from her bag and puts it over the shirt to hide the jut of her chest. She wraps her hair up in a bun and places our husband's wide-brimmed hats on top.

She steps inside the saloon. In the lantern-lit darkness she looks not so different from the other patrons. She walks with heavy, deliberate steps and sidles up to the game when there is a pause in the playing. Pushing a stool close, she sits and puts down her money in the center. She does not speak. For the first time in all my watching, I see her shoulders lower, her face loosen. She is happy now, free, perhaps as only a man can be, and if only for this one silent and dark night, recklessly throwing money into the pot, sloshing back the contents of her flask and shaking her head side to side as the liquid courses down her throat. I remember the saloon from before, when I was living, when I was in a body, but I can't recall the specifics. Did I sit on a stool at the bar and drink? Did I watch from the window? Did I pass by, hurrying to get somewhere else, and barely glance up at the façade? It was so long ago. So very, very long ago. The memory has frayed.

The game moves in a circle. The second wife throws cards down on the table. The man beside her with a thick beard and an angular, almost angry face slaps her on the back. She smiles a wide grin. The cards rain down, fast and faster. A fat man on the other side of the table, red scar running the length of his neck, stands up and throws his chair at the wall, storms off, and the rest shout at him until he exits through the doors and into the pitch dark of the muddy street. The second wife sweeps money off the table and into the deep pocket of her pants. The coins clank against the gun. The game continues, round and round.

It is a beautiful thing, the way the men and the second wife who appears to be a man, for this sliver of time freed from herself and from her entrapment as a mother to a baby not fully hers, are arrayed around the table, throwing down everything they have for a chance at something. They are not hemmed in by smallness, by the aspirations of petty men. They have dreams. They have come to this place out west looking for expanse, not only physical but spiritual. They seek land and they seek a wider soul. The game is another expression of that hope. They will bet it all on this creased deck of cards just as they bet it all on the journey to the frontier. It's all one thing or the other. Boom or bust. Rich or destitute. Alive or dead. For them, there's nothing in between.

After the saloon empties, I trail the second wife down the path out of town. It's nearly dawn. We pass the doctor's cabin where my baby's brain floats in its jar. Through the window, it glows in the light of the oil lamp. I want to go to it. I want to tuck it under my nonexistent arm and bring it home to the dybbuk baby as proof of something—I'm not sure what. The second wife moves quickly. Maybe she can sense the pull the brain exerts in our direction and wants to outrun it. I stay with her. I don't trust her.

Back home, she slinks inside before our husband wakes. She immediately sets about with her chores: scrubbing yesterday's bacon grease from the cast-iron skillet, emptying the chamber pot. A streak of shit clings to the bottom and she wipes it clean with the edge of her hand. She is back in the realm of woman, of wife and mother. Maybe she needs to keep busy to avoid looking at the baby, our baby, with those sharp eyes. I wait above, in the slats. She's grown better at ignoring my presence. From the way she pauses and glances in my direction from time to time, I know she feels it still, only that it has become almost natural to her, part of her. The tightness in the air where I float is like a ring, worn so often it's easy to forget it's not part of the skin.

Did the night in the saloon give her what she was searching for? Or has the brief respite only made her tenure here in the cabin with the baby and our husband more unbearable? Does she seek the kind of end that the jailer's wife spoke of with such resolve? Her eyes rim with red but she doesn't yawn.

I envy her whatever relief she felt. There is none for me. I get no rest. I do not get drunkenness or sleep or dreams. I am always who I am. I am always what I am. I can see no end to this. No way out. It occurs to me that if I were to be suddenly freed from this state, snapped out of my perch floating above the second wife and my husband and the dybbuk baby, I do not know what I would be. What is a ghost without a purpose? I am tethered, because to be tethered to another is to exist. Without the pull of the baby, I would cease to exist.

The second wife picks up an empty jar and holds it above the ground, then flings open her hand. It shatters on the ground. The fragments fly and one lands not far from the cradle. She stands above the jagged glass and stares. She doesn't move towards the broom. She doesn't lean down to gather the pieces.

My husband tosses in the bed. The baby gurgles in its cradle. I float over to be sure he is alright, to see if he has anything to say. He emits a fine film of bubbly spit across its lips, reaches a clenched fist up into the air and moves it back and forth, slowly, a knock on an invisible door. He is trying to be let in somewhere. He is trying to reach through to something or someone.

He gurgles again and, from deep within the baby, the dybbuk looks straight at me. It only lasts for a moment, but long enough for me to know he sensed a sliver of me in the air above. If I were embodied, and if he had his own body instead of tenancy in the body of another, I know that our eyes would have locked and we would have looked into each other, truly, for the first time, like real a mother and son.

Chicago

It's late morning by the time we arrive home. We park behind the apartment and carry Jonah up two flights of concrete stairs, or rather Jed carries him and I walk behind; I don't trust myself not to fall. I've already hurt him once, and these steps would be unforgiving. In the hospital we had nowhere to carry him. We lifted him out of the glass box and sat with him in the chair. He had to stay connected to his monitors. The nurses kept watch.

We continue up and up, out of breath by the time we summit. We open the door and walk in. Years after *Godspell*, I gave up musicals for orchestra because I was old enough to understand that I couldn't sing or dance or act. I had crossed through one of the Eriksonian thresholds, into adolescence, and with it came this bittersweet self-awareness. Afternoons I walked my viola up the steps into the practice room and unloaded the instrument from its case and greased the bow in rosin and played as the conductor waved her baton. We practiced in the crypt of a Catholic church, remains of nuns stored in drawers like kitchen utensils. Once, I dropped my instrument, still new, and the wood cracked like an egg on the stone floor. The bridge holding up the strings shattered. A crack slithered alongside the fingerboard. It got repaired but wasn't the same.

That first afternoon home we watch Jonah's fingers flicker, chest shiver, while he sleeps. He sits in the bouncer friends lent us months before, along with a bottle warmer still in its box and black trash bags filled with newborn clothes already too small, shoved on the top shelf of the nursery closet. The night before, Jed pulled the bassinet back out and placed it beside our bed yet again, but we don't put him there, not yet. Jonah opens his eyes, deep-sea blue, watches back, unblinking. His eyes do not let us wander. Jed and I sit on the floor next to him. *We have a baby*, we say out loud, over and over, to each other, to the fridge, to the fireplace, to anything whether or not it can listen. If we repeat it enough, maybe this time he will be ours. He will cease to be a baby of the hospital. He will shed the last remnants of the viscous glue that refuses to unstick from his scalp, which is the last reminder of its predecessor, the blue cap, that was actually more white than blue. Jonah has been through many stages of disguise. As we shear the layers away, he can become fully ours. At least that's the hope.

Reperfusion, we learned in the early days of the NICU, refers to the second stage of hypoxic injury. During the first—the tightening, the perceived moment of crisis—sufficient blood and oxygen fails to reach the brain. Then, as blood returns to withered neurons, waking stunned slabs of tissue, it shocks with an overabundance the fragile cells cannot handle in their half-wake state, a sudden surge onto parched land ill-equipped to absorb the excess. The long-awaited flood strikes worse than the drought. The three days and nights in the cap were an attempt to shield the brain from this flood, to stanch the gush. The treatment, doctors told us, must be initiated within six hours of birth. Otherwise, reperfusion has already begun, and once it starts the process can't be halted. Jonah, I learn through the medical records, began his cooling at 5.5 hours of life, sneaking in right under the cut-off.

Reperfusion wouldn't occur without the initial devastation, but the secondary blow's existence is more of an insult, a betrayal. The crisis should be over, the body removed from the offending circumstance. Yet it's a temporary break that lulls the body into a false peace. The second injury devastates because with it comes the knowledge that we now crouch forever in shadow, waiting for the next wave, and the next.

Science has no name for this. I'm not sure literature does either. The surprise assault of reperfusion means Jonah's story refuses to adhere to the neat diagram of Freytag's pyramid. There's rising action, crisis, falling action—then scramble. Rising action and portent of crisis rears out of falling action, denies denouement, absents resolution(s).

We're so glad that Jonah is home, friends exclaim. *What a relief it must be to have him out of the hospital and sleeping in his own bed. We're thrilled for your new little family!* They insist on discharge as demarcation, as narrative coda. Like the notion of luck, the trope of plot has a way of weaseling itself into places it doesn't belong. Plot tries to dull the edge of the unknown, or at least scaffold onlookers, standing on the other side of our glass box, as they watch us scrambling inside.

At the beginning of Nella Larsen's *Passing,* someone flicks cigarette ash out of an apartment window and watches the red flakes fall to the ground. At the end, one woman pushes another out of that window; the body plummets to pavement. There's a plotted, beautiful nature to the progression. I read it in the same high-school writing class where I read *Lolita*, and it struck me as exactly the way a story should work: one image, meaningless at first, becomes pure meaning by the end. The cigarette didn't need to reappear on the page for it to permeate. The blue cap may be our version of the cigarette, technically absent but permeating the rest of our pages.

A question persists: Were the three days of cooling a pause button pressed and released, or did the blue cap alter Jonah's course in the liminal space between birth and breath, cold and warmth, hospital and home? Is he the same baby as the one who emerged from the black box? Infants change at a rapid clip—their eyes start out so undeveloped they can't see much beyond a grayish blur; their floppy necks have to be supported at all times; they have no conception of themselves as separate from their caregivers nor of object permanence—and swiftly, over a jumble of days and nights, the changes pile up. They learn to sit and crawl and point at toys in the distance and cry out for a parent who has left the room. We call it growth and development, the stuff of child psychology that Erikson breaks down into digestible stages, and don't dwell on what it means about the stability of a person as an entity. A person isn't the same as a character, identified by a few key lines of description, endowed with a set of established traits, in the same way that life refuses to follow the rules of rising action and falling action.

One of my first acts as a mother to a baby in my own home is to throw out the copy of *What to Expect: The First Year.* I am angry at myself for buying it ahead of time and tempting fate—the ayin hara, perhaps, with the purchase; I'm furious with the authors whose cheerily upbeat lists of milestones and suggested activities and parenting tips organized by month taunts. The book presupposes a plot, neatly organized by month, that doesn't match our version of parenthood in the slightest. Jonah may not meet these milestones, or he may meet them late or scrambled out of order. We don't know. For us, the book's suggested activities get replaced by instructions from his team of therapists who come to our house and sit with him on the living room floor, dangling toys out of reach so he will lift his head or reach across the midline. I can expect nothing concrete except that I will have to wait and see for the future to be revealed. The name of the book alone is an insult.

I'm also angry at its predecessor, the original *What to Expect When You're Expecting,* for omitting our outcome as a possibility and instead promising a tidy, wrapped-up ending that never came to pass. *What are they supposed to do?* Jed asks when I complain about being misled, *scare every mother by discussing the remote possibility of brain injury?* To me, plopped into a life that doesn't seem to be mine anymore, that seems reasonable enough. I feel I've been sold a lie, as though my ignorance was the fault of some shady conglomerate comprised of OBs and doulas and authors of pregnancy books and the CEO of BuyBuy Baby. Big Birthing instead of Big Pharma, out to trick the unsuspecting consumer. Now that we're home, I can sort through the trash I've been sold and find my own way.

Over weeks I begin to get used to Jonah's cry and feel a twinge in my gut when I hear it down the hall, a reminder that the sound belongs to my baby and so I need to go to it. There's a chance I'm feeling the beginning tugs of a motherhood not bound up entirely with dread and despair and a throbbingly useless guilt that has padded around behind me like a nagging dog these stretched-out weeks, but it's too early to say for sure.

In the hospital, Jonah's cry started out silent, all effort and no result—a gape stuck on mute. Eventually, it gained force and sound, mingling with those of the other babies, difficult to distinguish from the pack. His cry would bring up unanswerable questions, as did seemingly every other aspect of his being. Doctors debated whether his voice was hoarse from prolonged intubation or the thick, inhaled meconium liquor still mucking up his lungs or some cocktail of the two. The thick green from the water breaking had to be filtered from the pink tissue, a slow process I did not fully understand, except that I knew, by this point, that water breaking does not end.

When biblical Jonah reached shore at last, spit out and his journey nearly complete, perhaps he noticed a heaviness to his breath, the inhaled sea not fully cleared, sloshing around in his lungs, a thick sputum. He would cough to clear his throat, tasting the briny remnants that had become part of him, same as his blood and nails and skin. He would never truly leave the ocean behind.

When he's deep in sleep, I notice an irregularity to Jonah's inhales, a jaggedness in the pauses. Over the phone, the on-call pediatrician, irritated at having been pulled away from dinner for nothing, tells me this is normal newborn physiology—periodic breathing. *Their respiration is immature*, she says. *They are still learning how to breathe.* The body, I come to understand, takes its time transitioning from circulation of the womb to circulation in the world. Even so, the pauses between inhales become moments of fleeting panic while I wait for the return of rhythm. There's no such thing as normal. I'll always be waiting.

Back at that coffee shop before Jonah, eavesdropping on the doula, I thought of birth as a mere sliver of time—a few hours, perhaps a day, beginning when contractions start and ending with a baby placed on one's chest. And yet now, home, this day lurks, a handful of hours staring down at me from the microwave when I remove my steaming coffee cup or up from the trucks idling in the alley out back. I'm standing in the kitchen staring at a dishrag and I'm in the delivery room. The nurse is counting out contractions. I'm pushing, and the forceps are pulling. Jonah cries. I can't look away from the dishrag, balled up and stuck with bits of food. His pacifier, I imagine, has tumbled. I can't go to him because the dishrag is a magnet, pulling me back to the hospital, to its winding halls and elevators and containment rooms with double doors. I'm stuck in the water breaking that never ends, the three days expanded to four.

Doctors reassure us that the brain is the one organ spared pain. They say this with certainty. It's the one comfort they can offer: Jonah's injury hasn't hurt him, whatever else it has done and will do. I want to know if this is the same kind of pain-sparing that natural birthing books claim when they describe labor for the *right* sort of mother, which isn't really pain-sparing at all but teeth-gritting in the hopes of satisfying some vague ideal of womanhood.

I think about devising a Freytag's triangle for labor and delivery and what comes after. This new version would flatten and loop to represent a plot comprised not of rising and falling action, conflict followed by resolution, but of contractions bleeding together and water breaking that never ends and a delivery that seems like an ending but instead sends the protagonist back to start, to the doors of the hospital with the signing doorman, trapped in iterative action. It would be based on the malleable nature of time—the new, baggy time, time transformed during the three days in the cap, time I am still trying to acclimate to. Now, home, the plot continues. I keep searching for the denouement, but it's nowhere to be found. This is not a short story, and now I know that becoming a mother is to enter this winding house of mirrors or a time machine or both.

A series of disconnected vignettes comprises the story of *Godspell*'s Jesus. In between Jesus's opening baptism and his mournful solo in the Garden of Gethsemane, the cast performs the parable of Lazarus, enacts the story of the prodigal son, pretends to be a flock of straying goats cast down to hell. The structure is linear—beginning with John the Baptist, ending with the crucifixion and death—and also scattered, based on theme and moral, not temporal sequence.

Returning from one of our first walks, Jonah burrowed in his stroller, I close my eyes as we pass the yoga studio on the ground floor of our building. Hold my breath, 1, 2, 3, enter the stairwell, 4, 5, 6. Release. *Don't look,* I warn Jonah, the way I once told him to shield his ears from the shouting parents of the healthiest baby in the NICU. Is the instructor rising from lotus pose at the front of the dimly lit room, approaching each mother-to-be and placing a gentle palm on their shoulders, pulling their necks taut, opening up the spaces for them to send their love energies to their babies? So much has changed and also nothing at all. The rest of the world keeps going and going, as though the blue cap never happened.

The quiet of our bedroom unnerves me. There is no constant chime of monitors announcing that the baby's heart rate or oxygen level has dipped, no nurses lurking behind curtains and sliding doors. No strange inbreeding of anxiety and comfort where everything is at once terribly chaotic—on the verge of catastrophe—and completely under control. There is no other mother with stringy, bleached hair and fat, red toes fretting over her twins in the next bay. No family protesting the hospital's rules that have unfairly landed their healthy baby in the land of the sick. There is nothing but me and the baby lying beside me, two bodies that have failed each other once trying to start over, and the thump thump thump of his heartbeat. Sometimes his breathing pauses—periodic breathing, I remind myself—and starts up again. Thump thump thump, goes his heartbeat. He is still here. This is by turns calming and terrifying. I switch the TV on to something mindless to distract myself. Some procedural drama where the ending is clear from the episode's start. But how can I watch a show when I've finally got my baby home? How can I do anything other than stare? I turn it off.

I pick Jonah up from his bassinet and hold him against my chest while he sleeps so I can feel the way his heartbeat tells me he's still there. It's my way, also, of telling him I'm sorry.

I'm alive, it says, *I'm alive.*

Yes, yes you are, I say, to convince myself this steadiness will remain. That I'm okay suspended in continuous waiting for an ending that won't come. The blue cap will linger, unlike the body in *Passing* that falls from the window, fulfilling the promise of the cigarette.

At each visit, the pediatrician measures Jonah's head. *Hello handsome,* she says, commenting on his bright eyes. The circumference is not growing at the expected rate, the line on the growth chart plateauing. Things are not going according to the plot outlined by the CDC. She points to her computer screen where Jonah's dots form a faulty Freytag's triangle. The line connecting them only rises a bit and then levels off. It doesn't reach the climax it's supposed to. *But there's nothing to do*, she says. She explains that it's simply evidence of the injury we know occurred. An artifact. She asks about his fluid intake. It's not unheard of, I learn scrolling through online support groups, for brain-damaged babies to eat by mouth at first and then, when the sucking reflex dissipates and the higher brain must take over. The water sloshes at the edges of our boat, sometimes lopping up onto the deck. The sea is fitful and unpredictable, God angry at Jonah for running away, and we will have to try to steer the ship around it all. We can't toss him overboard.

When I performed in *Godspell*, I could hardly believe the physicality of that god, skin pierced through with nails, body drooped. I couldn't imagine a Jewish god with a punctured, bleeding body. The Jewish god was a disembodied voice echoing out over the desert. He promised an ethereal messiah who would never materialize. This god came to people as fragments of dreams, or when they were delirious with hunger or heat or exhaustion, and then stopped appearing at all. I saw a foreign kind of ecstatic joy on the faces of the Christian kids when they closed their eyes and grinned as the cast formed a circle and held hands to pray before the show. Their god was real and solid, evidenced by his gasping, writhing death. Their god had a conclusion. Mine: barely there, and withholding any tidy end, especially the dramatic kind of Jesus' death and resurrection.

Jonah, in a way, has been resurrected. Born not breathing, doctors resuscitated him in the delivery room. But the resurrection was medical and not miraculous, and he has no triumphant, Christian return. His trajectory is fitful and continuous. *I'm alive, I'm alive,* Jonah's heartbeat utters to me. I put him down in the bassinet and moments later he's up again crying, demanding I hold him. Up/down, up/down we go. What if the brain injury is deeper than we thought, that it's interrupting the most basic of his body's duties— sleep? *I'm alive, I'm alive, I'm alive,* his heartbeat says in response, once he's back on my chest. We're stuck in a Jewish god-like loop.

When I breastfeed Jonah I time how long he sucks on each side, moving a hair elastic from one wrist to the next to remember which breast he last ate from, which nipple I last unhitched his mouth from by inserting the tip of my pinkie to break the seal the way the NICU nurses showed me. Tracking his eating is key because women apparently produce varieties of milk—foremilk and hindmilk—and the nutrient-dense milk is in the hindmilk, which only comes out at the end, once the baby has nearly emptied the breast. My meager pumping output means I need to top him off with formula from a bottle. Twice a day we have to mix his deep red phenobarbital in with the formula. Phenobarbital is sedating, so we try to feed him this before his naps and avoid it for the hour or so before his scheduled physical or occupational therapy. What should be the simple task of feeding becomes a complex web that needs to be tracked and plotted.

When I read *Passing* so many years ago, I was struck by how Nella Larsen's ash preceded body, placed a frame of expectation around plod of event. The book seemed to hold its breath from that glowing image until it finally exhaled at the fall.

Now I'm not a high schooler hunched over my creased paperback, highlighter in hand, jotting notes in the margins as my teacher lectures. Now there is a flutter of red ash from the window without the subsequent body, or the plummet of body without the preceding ash. There's a normal pregnancy that ends with a baby in a blue cap. There are the healthy infants born after their fetal monitoring strips sound alarms. Event without warning. Warning without event. There is no plot.

In time I begin to tell my story, and once I do, I can't seem to stop. It's hardly a story, more a jumble of emotions. I tell it to the mother pushing her baby in the park swing who nods politely and fumbles for a new subject. I can't look directly at her baby because, like the stroller in the hotel's elevator bank, the swing holding this other child is a force field repelling my glance. When I accidentally glimpse the edge of the baby's foot, the blood rushes too fast to my head, a reminder of the story I thought I'd be telling and the one I am. I tell my story to the teacher of the baby music class as she puts away her guitar, and the hair stylist as she snips away at my bangs. Phrases tumble from me without my consent. I do not know why the words emerge. There I go again: on the train, in the zoo, at the party. I must be trying to piece it together, to understand the order of its elements and its causal structure, to root out agency and plumb guilt, but I'm only dimly aware that I'm engaged in this crude meaning-making. Mostly it's an automatic narration. This is my story but also not my story. I have no control over its contours. It falls out of me and I leave it behind like a skin shed across the city.

Again and again we return to the hospital for EEGs. We climb the too-tight lanes of the too-crowded parking garage, receive our ID badges from the security station. Inside, techs dot Jonah's head in electrodes, and then doctors read sentences of lines and spikes, paragraphs of dips and resurgences on the screen. In medicine many results are said to be read but that is, often, a misnomer. An X-ray or MRI is a static image regarded like a painting in a gallery. But an EEG leaves behind a swoop of brainwaves moving through space and time. There is plot; there is a beginning and middle and end, arbitrarily determined by application and removal of sensors, but present, nonetheless. Within this framework there is an arc or series of arcs and when an abnormal spike or seizure strikes there is crisis—the most basic diagram of the most basic sort of story. This is as close as we come to a Fretyagian plot.

Doctors are watching for a form of epilepsy that they warn children with brain injuries are at risk for. The rug might get pulled out from under us again. We must monitor, wait. The signs we are looking for seem innocent to the untrained eye, but they warn us not to be lulled. Like the second stage of hypoxic injury, this syndrome can sneak in, undetected until it has already wreaked havoc. Another kind of reperfusion. We can't seem to break free of the loop, to find our exit. The messiah is not coming.

In between our hospital visits I spend entire days in bed, Jonah suctioned to my chest. He still refuses to sleep if I put him down. I like to think he's making up for lost time. *I'm alive,* he says with his heartbeat. *I'm alive.*

I'm your mother, I say back. *I'm your mother. The blue cap was just a blue cap. It contains no deeper meaning. Don't think about it anymore.* But when he closes his eyes and I stare at his sides to make sure his organs are still pumping blood throughout his body, the blue cap is all I see.

Ninevah, sin-filled city God ordered Jonah to visit, to warn, is situated in the northern corner of modern-day Iraq, bordering Syria and Turkey. Names change but beneath new dust is old. It never goes away.

After one EEG, the doctor describes the misfirings of Jonah's brain as orchestral instruments playing out of step with the conductor's baton. Where there should be unison and harmony there is discord. I see him reaching for another metaphor and ask a question to halt the onslaught. He's like a modern-day William Smellie—ramrod-ding his way through, to where he isn't welcome. This is a new use for questions, I've discovered—the question mark as a deflection, a reorientation, a way for me to sneak in and claim control.

The yoga teacher's practice rested on the notion that prior states can be reinhabited. *As you come out of shavasana*, she whispered, *let your limbs feel their way back into themselves. Let your breath reenter your lungs. Let your thoughts return to your mind. Reacquaint yourself with your baby.*

No! I want to shout at her now, if I could muster the strength to return to the studio. *Liar!* A body cannot go back to what it was before. I'm as stuck as the baby in the cooling cap. I can't reclaim the person I inhabited pre-Jonah. As I walk around the apartment, trying to comfort a fussy baby with rhythmic steps and bounces, I picture the women she's indoctrinating below. The yoga instructor is also part of Big Birthing, one of its many seemingly innocuous spokes spouting their propaganda. I realize I may be going overboard, that maybe she's not as malicious as all that, maybe she just wants to help pregnant women with their aches and pains, but I need a place to deposit my rage.

In time I learn the limits of the EEG. What it can see: electrical activity emitted from lobes of brain, cells firing in concert or not. What it can't: spark beneath it all, or smoldering ash—the source of rogue jags of lightning—and the way these rogue jags will or will not accumulate into storms. It can read chapters of a book but can't predict the epilogue.

At some point God stops intervening in history, stops speaking to the Israelites with commands and invectives and warnings, stops appearing in the flames of burning bushes and the ladders of dreams. The revelations halt for unidentified reasons and God recedes into the landscape. A divine developmental regression, like what doctors warn the dreaded seizures can cause. Theologians come up with all sorts of clever justifications for this shift, much like their recalibration of biblical time in accordance with modern scientific discoveries like dinosaur fossils. The obvious conclusion, though, is that the revelations never happened in the first place, and that our ancestors made up this surreal dialogue with God to instill the vast emptiness with power and meaning. This mythmaking is unreliable memory on a grand scale, altering communal reality with a shared delusion. The story I'm trying to tell to the other mom and the music teacher and hair stylist is my attempt at personal mythmaking based on unreliable memory. I want to unearth the fragments and place them side by side. They don't really fit together, but I try anyway. There's no way to make what happened make sense. I am creating a delusion.

My postpartum state involves moments of stark disjunction from my body, perhaps a splitting that began in the delivery room when I found myself in the vent. I walk down the street and feel a hot spoke of sun on my shoulder. The skyline shimmers to the east. I am suddenly, out of nowhere, happy in a way I haven't been in months. Then I feel tears on my cheeks, and I'm unsure if the tears follow from the physical shock of bright late summer light or from some furious backlog of emotion my unexpected happiness has unplugged.

I stop in the middle of the sidewalk. Cars churn past at the light, a driver presses into her horn, clients enter the yoga studio, kids shout on the school playground, run towards and away from each other. I used to be one of the pregnant clients entering the yoga studio, and I thought I was on my way to having one of those children on the playground, though now I'm not sure. My vision is blurred and the sounds are muffled. The world is like Jonah's silent scream when he first began to cry. I'm caught in what amounts to the transition phase, not quite a mother and not quite not a mother, confronting the dawning realization that there is no resolution.

At our periodic visits to the Hawaiian-shirted neurologist, we ask variations on the theme of *Who is our baby.* The doctor digs for something in a coat pocket and does not look us in the eye. He clicks the top of a pen, rubs his hands together with sanitizer from the pump near the door. What we really want to know is something he can't answer: is the real baby the one before or after the injury? Or are these two babies somehow contained in the same body?

Back home, I pour water on Jonah's hair with a pink plastic cup. He splashes a hand to the surface and sends lukewarm droplets raining down his cheek. In the kitchen, pans clatter and music plays.

Do you remember what was there before? Who you were? I ask. Jonah stares up at me, seals his lips. I feel guilty for imagining the inside of his head as pocked and injured. For imposing the concept of time, of a before and after. *I am that I am, God* announced to Moses from the bush, before he stopped revealing himself in history.

Suds foam on Jonah's forehead. I wipe them away from his eyes. The bottle promises no tears but I want to err on the side of caution, of not causing any more suffering.

You can tell me, I say to him, scrubbing behind his ears and under his chin. *Whatever it is you want to tell me, it's okay.* Lately his face has begun to take on the shape of a baby's rather than a newborn's; when he smiles his cheeks pucker and reveal deep dimples and his blue eyes glisten with recognition.

I hold his chubby arm to keep him from sliding down under the surface, but the soap forms a slick on his skin and I am afraid my grip will slip. Jonah looks up at me, wide-eyed and now open-mouthed. I see something gurgling in him, a faint flutter in his chest and neck, a twitch of his lips—the beginnings of a reply—but he closes his lips before an answer slips out. *Not yet,* he seems to wink. Or is he flinching at a water drop?

Nothing is certain, the neurologist warned us that day when I lay flat on the plastic sofa of the family meeting room. He perched the MRI results, which seemed to contain the key to this child, still a stranger, on the shelf of his stomach. Jonah, ultimately, would have to show us the answers, the doctor explained. More waiting felt unbearable. The neurologist asked if we had questions. In the pause I could hear Jed's quick breath next to me.

It's time, I announce to Jonah as he happily flutters his feet. I take out the stopper and watch the soapy water begin to eddy down the drain, lift him out and wrap him in his yellow towel. He feels solid in my arms, more and more so each day.

I will, eventually, get a revelation—my booming-voiced, God-on-the-mountaintop moment. After months of trying to coax sounds and words out of Jonah to no avail, after we blow past the deadlines set by *What to Expect* and the pediatrician's developmental checklist, he will finally decide to speak. Before, he sat flattened under too much medication, the heavy-duty stuff we had to inject in his thigh and a second drug delivered via a specialty pharmacy, both prescribed when he was in fact diagnosed with the destructive form of epilepsy the doctors warned of. We will get lucky; the drugs will work and his brain waves will calm. We will wean him, and he will start to wake up, to look at us, more and more alert. From his crib-side monitor, I will begin to hear strings of babbles as he practices—*lalala dadada*. I will stay up listening to his voice. Then, one morning he will climb onto his Sesame Street couch and point to the picture on the front. *Elmo,* he will say, as though it's the most natural thing in the world.

Skip ahead, many more years in the future. I will hear Jonah shouting to his friend from atop a hill as they play chase. He will trip, laugh, get up, keep running. *Five minutes!* I will shout. Jonah will run faster. As he disappears behind a crop of trees, I will catch the glimmer of his blue cap, of the strap taut underneath his chin. I'll lift off the bench nestled in this quiet suburban park and find myself deposited years earlier, on the busy street in front of our old apartment, frozen on the concrete between the yoga studio and the elementary school where kids play on the slide and swings, usure if I'll find my way out from my liminal postpartum state and become a full mother to a full child. Traffic will barrel past.

 Five minutes, I will repeat, landing back in the quiet of the leafy park, hands clutching the damp wooden slats beneath me. It will be getting late. Empty swings will stutter in the evening wind and the basketball posts' shadows will stretch long and thin. Jonah will emerge from behind the trees and, still running, tilt his head slightly in the direction of my voice.

Acknowledgements

Thank you to Barrelhouse, and my amazing, dedicated editors, Lilly Dancyger and Lindsey Trout Hughes, for taking a leap of faith on this project, and believing in its weirdness. I am so grateful for your keen insights, which made this book truer to itself.

Thank you to my teachers at SAIC and elsewhere, who helped shape me as a writer. Special thanks to Janet Desaulniers, for always seeing straight through to the heart of the work, and for continuing to read drafts and offer feedback and support long after my graduation; and to Sara Levine for telling me early on that there was something to the kernels that would eventually become this book, for encouraging me to keep at it when the going got tough, and for the patient and practical career advice.

To my fellow Chicago writers, especially Suman Chhabra, Rebecca Nakaba, and Emily Maloney, for the incisive feedback and companionship as I wrote this, searched for a home for it, and embarked on edit after edit.

To the Vermont Studio Center and the Virginia Center for Creative Arts for providing crucial time and space for me to write, and to the other writers and artists I met in residence. You inspired me with your work and encouraged me in mine. Thank you to the editors at *Mississippi Review* who gave an early excerpt from the book a home.

To the medical staff and therapists who took excellent care of Jonah and helped him grow into the kid he is today, but especially to Jody Schaaf, for making sure we could see the light at the end of the tunnel.

To my friends, too many to list, who provided such crucial love and support. Thank you for the meals and company on tough days, the lake walks, the personalized medical expertise, the apartment hallway tangos with a cranky baby, and so much more. Some people say that friendships strain once you have kids, but I experienced the total opposite.

To my family: Jackie and Chuck Stern, Rebecca and Matthew Stern (and Bina), Lily Stern, Eleanor Stern and Jonah Goldman Kay, Emma Stern; and Sydney Kase and Scott Glickstein, Sophie Glickstein and Jermaine Affonso (and Otis), and Lily Glickstein. You swooped in on day one—from New Orleans and Minnesota, Boston and even Vietnam—without us having to ask, and never left our side. You made it clear that no matter what we faced we would not be alone, which in turn made it bearable, and eventually joyful and beautiful, to keep chugging. A special shout-out to Eleanor for making sure I'm not the sole writer in the family, and for patiently fielded lots of neurotic calls throughout the book-making process.

Most of all:

To Jed, for climbing in next to me at the beginning, for believing in me, for taking over on many nights and weekends so I could work, and for being a true partner in every sense of the word.

To Isaac and Nathan, extraordinary brothers and sons.

And to Jonah: your answers were worth the wait.

Sources & Influences

Books

Berlin, Adele, Brettler, Marc Zvi, and Fishbane, Michael, editors. *The Jewish Study Bible*. New York: Oxford University Press, 2004.

Bretler, Marc Z., Newsom, Carol A., and Perkins, Pheme, editors. *The New Oxford Annotated Bible, Third Edition*. New York: Oxford University Press, 2001.

Brown, Dee. *The Gentle Tamers: Women of the Old West*. New York: Putnam, 1958.

Brown, Dee. *Wondrous Times on the Frontier*. Little Rock: August House Publishers, Inc., 1991.

Dexter, Pete. *Deadwood*. New York: Random House, Inc., 1986.

Dick-Read, Grantly. *Childbirth Without Fear: New Fourth Edition* (Rev. and Ed. by Helen Wessel and Harlan F. Ellis). New York: Harper & Row, 1979.

Erikson, Eric. *Childhood and Society*. New York: W.W. Norton & Co., 1950.

Gies, Frances and Joseph. *Life in a Medieval Village*. New York: Harper, 1990.

Goodrich, Frederick W., Jr. *Natural Childbirth: A Manual for Expectant Parents*. Englewood Cliffs, NJ: Prentice-Hall Inc., 1950.

Leavitt, Judith Walzer. *Brought to Bed: Child-Bearing in America, 1750-1950*. Oxford University Press, 1988.

Miles, Jack. *God: A Biography*. New York: Alfred A. Knopf, 1995.

Nuegroschel, Joachim (Ed. Tr). *Great Tales of Jewish Fantasy and the Occult: The Dybbuk and Thirty Other Classic Stories.* Woodstock and New York: The Overlook Press, 1987.

Rich, Adrienne. *Of Woman Born: Motherhood as Experience and Institution.* New York: W.W. Norton & Co., 1976.

Scovil, Elisabeth Robinson. *Preparation for Motherhood.* Philadelphia: Henry Altemus, 1896.

Wertz, Richard W., and Wertz, Dorothy C. *Lying-In: A History of Childbirth in America.* New Haven: Yale University Press, 1989.

Articles, Podcasts, and Websites

Astington, Janet Wilde, and Edward, Margaret J. "Early Development of Theory of Mind in Early Childhood." *Social Cognition,* August 2010, https://www.child-encyclopedia.com/pdf/expert/social-cognition/according-experts/development-theory-mind-early-childhood.

Coy, Peter. "When Being Good is Just a Matter of Being Lucky." *The New York Times:* 20 September 2023, https://www.nytimes.com/2023/09/20/opinion/moral-luck.html.

Dickstein, Stephanie. "Jewish Ritual Practice Following a Stillbirth." *Rabbinic Assembly,* https://www.vox.com/the-gray-area/23965798/free-will-robert-sapolsky-determined-the-gray-area.

Domonoske, Camilla. "'Father of Gynecology,' Who Experimented on Slaves, No Longer on Pedestal In NYC," *The Two Way,* NPR, 17 April, 2018, https://www.npr.org/sections/thetwo-way/2018/04/17/603163394/-father-of-gynecology-who-experimented-on-slaves-no-longer-on-pedestal-in-nyc.

Eberly, Susan Schoon. "Fairies and the Folklore of Disability: Changelings, Hybrids and the Solitary Fairy." *Folklore,* vol. 99. no.1, 1988, pp. 58-77.

"Erik Erikson." *Encyclopedia Brittanica,* https://www.britannica.com/biography/Erik-Erikson.

Fleming, James S. "Erikson's Psychosocial Developmental Stages." *Psychological Perspectives on Human Development,* 2004, http://swppr.org/textbook/Ch%201%20Intro.pdf.

Gawande, Atul. "The Score: How Childbirth Went Industrial. *The New Yorker,* 2005.

Goldstein, Yaakov. "The Laws & Customs of Mourning Vol. 1." *The passing of an infant, Nefel, stillborn & miscarriage.* Safed, Israel: 2019, https://shulchanaruchharav.com/halacha/chapter-10-the-passing-of-an-infant-nefel-stillborn-miscarriage/.

Hammer, Jill, "Lilith: Lady Flying in Darkness: The most notorious demon of Jewish tradition becomes a feminist hero" *My Jewish Learning,* https://www.myjewishlearning.com/article/lilith-lady-flying-in-darkness/.

Herzog, Lena, Photographs: "Incompatible with Life." *The Paris Review,* 188. New York, New York, Spring 2009.

Holland, Brynn, "The 'Father of Modern Gynecology' Performed Shocking Experiments on Enslaved Women." *History,* A&E Television Networks, 29 August 2017, https://www.history.com/news/the-father-of-modern-gynecology-performed-shocking-experiments-on-slaves.

Homan, Maura, "How this Black doctor is exposing the racist history of gynecology." *Today,* 20 June 2020, https://www.today.com/health/racism-gynecology-dr-james-marion-sims-t185269.

Illing, Sean, host. "The Case Against Free Will." *The Gray Area,* Vox. 21 November 2023, https://www.vox.com/the-gray-area/23965798/free-will-robert-sapolsky-determined-the-gray-area.

Kalogeris, Theodore, Baines, Christopher P., Krenz, Maike, and Korthuis, Ronald J. "Cell Biology of Ischemia/Reperfusion Injury." *International Review of Cell and Molecular Biology,* vol. 298, 2012, pp. 229-317.

Levingston, Steven. "Jackie Kennedy's Five Pregnancies: The Tragic and the Successful." *Huffington Post,* 23 Jan, 2014, http://www.huffingtonpost.com/steven-levingston/jackie-kennedys-five-pregnancies_b_4273416.html.

Michaelson, Jay, "Demons, Dybbuks, Ghosts, and Golems: Do Jews believe in demons?" My Jewish Learning: https://www.myjewishlearning.com/article/demons-dybbuks-ghosts-golems/.

Mosley, Tonya, host. "After a traumatic C-section, journalist takes on the medicalization of birth." *Fresh Air,* NPR, 28 May 2024.

Orenstein, Gabriel A. and Lewis, Lindsay. "Eriksons Stages of Psychosocial Development." *National Library of Medicine,* 7 November, 2022, https://www.ncbi.nlm.nih.gov/books/NBK556096/

Peliowski-Davidovich, Abraham; Canadian Paediatric Society, Fetus and Newborn Committee. "Hypothermia for newborns with hypoxic ischemic encephalopathy." *Pediatric Child Health,* 17:1, 2012, pp.41-43.

Pilkenton, Deanna, and Schorn, Mavis N. *Midwifery: A Career for Men in Nursing. Men In Nursing,* Februrary, 2008, https://nursing.vanderbilt.edu/msn/pdf/nmw_midwiferyformen.pdf.

"Rethinking the Legacy of Marion Sims." *Equal Justice Initiative,* 9 January 2023, https://eji.org/news/rethinking-the-legacy-of-marion-sims/.

Salmon-Mack, Tamar, Trans. Carrie Friedman-Cohen. "Birth and Birthing," *The YIVO Encyclopedia of Jewish in Eastern Europe,* YIVO Institute for Jewish Research, https://encyclopedia.yivo.org/article/2078

Sefaria Community Translation, *Unetaneh Tokef, https://www.sefaria.org/Unetaneh_Tokef.1?lang=bi&with=all&lang2=en.*

Sheikh, Sukhera, Ganesaratnam, Inithan, and Jan, Haider. "The Birth of Forceps." *Journal of the Royal Society of Medicine,* 4:7, 2013, pp.1-4.

Schorsch, Ismar. "Meaning in the Torah's Layout." *JTS Torah Archive,* 25 December, 1999, https://www.jtsa.edu/torah/meaning-in-the-torahs-layout/.

"The Six Wives of Henry VIII," http://www.pbs.org/wnet/sixwives/.

Telushkin, Joseph. "Chevra Kadisha, or the Jewish Burial Society." myjewishlearning.org.

University of Cambridge, "Medieval 'birthing girdle' parchment was worn during Labor, study suggests," *University of Cambridge,* March, 2021, https://www.cam.ac.uk/research/news/medieval-birthing-girdle-parchment-was-worn-during-labour-study-suggests.

Varghese, Binoj, Xavier, Rose, Manoj, VC, Aneesh MK Priya, PS, Kumar, Ashok and Sreenivasan, VK. "Magnetic resonance imaging spectrum of perinatal hypoxic ischemic brain injury." *Indian Journal of Radiology and Imagining*. 26(4):530, 2016, pp. 316–327.

Wiener, Sophie, "Jewish Word//Dybbuk." *Moment Magazine*, November-December, 2012, https://www.myjewishlearning.com/article/demons-dybbuks-ghosts-golems/.

Wolfson, Ron. "How to Mourn Stillbirth and Neonatal Death: New Jewish Guidelines for Coping with the Loss of a Child." *My Jewish Learning:* https://www.myjewishlearning.com/article/stillbirth-and-neonatal-death/.

About the Author

Erica Stern's work has been published in *The Iowa Review*, *Mississippi Review*, *Denver Quarterly*, and elsewhere. She has received support for her writing from the Vermont Studio Center and the Virginia Center for Creative Arts. A New Orleans native, she lives with her family in Evanston, Illinois.